The Rosary
Prayer by Prayer

The Rosary Prayer by Prayer

How and Why We Pray the Christ-Centered Rosary of the Blessed Mother

Mary K. Doyle

3E PRESS

Geneva, IL

Nihil Obstat: Charles McNamee, J.C.L.
Censor Librorum

Imprimatur: + Thomas G. Doran, D.D., J.C.D.
Bishop of Rockford

The Rosary Prayer by Prayer Copyright ©Mary K. Doyle, 2006. Cover Art and Illustrations ©Joseph Cannella, 2006. Published by 3E Press, Geneva, IL, 3epress@sbcglobal.net, Phone: 630-262-9064, Fax: 630-208-1034. All rights reserved. No part of this book, or parts thereof, may be reproduced or transmitted in any form or by any means, electronic or mechanical, including photocopying and recording, or by any information storage and retrieval system, without written permission from the copyright holder.
Printed and bound in the United States of America.
Luke 1:46-55 (*Magnificat*) in "Additional Prayers" is from the New Revised Standard Version of the Bible, copyright ©1989 by the Division of Christian Education of the National Council of the Churches of Christ in the U.S.A. Used by permission. All rights reserved.
Excerpts from the New American Bible with Revised New Testament and Psalms Copyright © 1991, 1986, 1970 Confraternity of Christian Doctrine, Inc, Washington, DC. Used with permission. All rights reserved. No portion of the New American Bible may be reprinted without permission in writing from the copyright holder.
The English translation of the Litany of the Blessed Virgin Mary from *Order of Crowning an Image of the Blessed Virgin Mary* © 1986, International Committee on English in the Liturgy, Inc. All rights reserved.
Excerpts from *Vatican Council II, Volume 1, Revised Edition: The Conciliar & Post Conciliar Documents,* edited by Rev. Austin Flannery, O.P. copyright 2003, Costello Publishing Company, Inc., Northport, NY are used by permission of the publisher, all rights reserved. No part of these excerpts may be reproduced, stored in a retrieval system, or transmitted in any form or by any means - electronic, mechanical, photocopying, recording or otherwise, without express permission of Costello Publishing Company, Inc.

Publisher's Cataloging-in-Publication
(Provided by Quality Books, Inc.)

Doyle, Mary K.
  The Rosary prayer by prayer : how and why we pray the Christ-centered Rosary of the Blessed Mother / Mary K. Doyle.
  p. cm.
  Includes bibliographical references and index.
  LCCN 2005903321
  ISBN-13: 978-0-9677449-3-3
  ISBN-10: 0-9677449-3-8
  ISBN-13: 978-0-9677449-4-0
  ISBN-10: 0-9677449-4-6

  1. Rosary.   I. Title.

BX2163.D69 2005   242'.74
                          QBI05-600022

DEDICATION

The Rosary Prayer by Prayer is dedicated to all who pray the rosary or have an interest in learning more about this devotion. May you always feel the presence and love of Jesus and Mary, and may your love for them grow with every prayer.

PRAYER BEFORE THE ROSARY

My dear Blessed Mother, please pray the holy rosary with me. Assist me with the prayers and reflections so that I may gain greater insight into the mysteries. Help me to keep an open mind and heart to the direction of our Father. Amen.

CONTENTS

Contents

ARTWORK
BY
JOSEPH CANNELLA

Cover Art:
Praying the Rosary/Oil on Wood Panel

Illustrations:
The Annunciation/Graphite
The Visitation/Graphite
The Nativity/Graphite
The Presentation/Graphite
The Finding in the Temple/Graphite
The Baptism of Jesus/Graphite
Jesus' First Miracle/Graphite
The Proclamation of the Kingdom/Graphite
The Transfiguration/Graphite
The Institution of the Eucharist/Graphite
The Agony in the Garden/Graphite
The Scourging at the Pillar/Graphite
The Crowning with Thorns/Graphite
The Carrying of the Cross/Graphite
The Crucifixion/Graphite
The Resurrection/Silver Point
The Ascension/Silver Point
The Descent of the Holy Spirit/Silver Point
The Assumption/Silver Point
The Coronation/Silver Point

ACKNOWLEDGMENTS

Thank you to everyone who expressed the need for a book that would clearly teach how to pray the rosary and also promote a deeper prayer experience for those who already cherish the rosary. This book was designed with you in mind.

My thanks to the many people who have been models of faith for me. Thank you to my parents, aunts and uncles, and the BVM sisters who taught me how to pray the rosary when I was a child. They showed me their devotion on a daily basis. Rev. Msgr Joseph Jarmoluk and Rev. Bernard (Bernie) LaMontagne are two priests who are special blessings to our Catholic Church. I am very thankful for their friendship, guidance, example, and their devotion to Mary. I also am thankful for the daily love and support of all of my family, especially my husband, Marshall Brodien.

Thank you to all of my teachers and fellow students at St. Mary-of-the-Woods College. The experience I had with them in pursuit of my Master's Degree in Pastoral Theology was life-changing. My theological foundation and faith has grown tremendously under their teachings, examples, and sharing of life experiences.

I sincerely thank St. Mary-of-the-Woods College Professor Father Bernie LaMontagne and St. Peter Catholic Church Adult Formation Director and Liturgical Minister Paul Fay and Coordinator for Adult Catechesis and RCIA Kristina Rake for assisting me with my Master's Degree pastoral project, "Mary and the Rosary."

The Rosary Prayer by Prayer

Kristina also has my gratitude for editing the manuscript for this book. Her theological and grammatical expertise was very valuable. Many thanks to Lisa Cannella, Erin Horonzy, Andrew Mariotti, Don Fish, and Brittany Gauss for posing for some of the illustrations. My thanks to Father Kurt Spengler and my dear friend, Jeanie Fentz, for sharing books that were very helpful with my research. Thank you to Erin Horonzy and Patricia Brewer for carefully proofreading the manuscript and offering suggestions on how it could be improved and to Virginia Unverzagt, D.Min., the Director of Graduate Programs in Pastoral Theology, St. Mary-of-the-Woods College for her comments. And a very special thank you to The Most Reverend Thomas G. Doran, D.D., J.C.D, Reverend Monsignor Charles McNamee, J.C.L., and the Reverend Monsignor Glenn L. Nelson, J.C.L. for the careful review of *The Rosary Prayer by Prayer*.

Most of all I thank my son, Joseph, for seeing this project through to completion. Producing the oil painting for the cover and 20 detailed illustrations was a daunting assignment for a young student. He worked diligently to comprehend the Scriptures relating to the mysteries, develop a fresh perspective, and create exceptional devotional art. His work adds tremendously to the book's potential for a heightened prayer experience.

The Rosary Prayer by Prayer

The Rosary Prayer by Prayer

PART I

HOW AND WHY

WE PRAY THE ROSARY

The Rosary Prayer by Prayer

THE ROSARY AND JESUS' GIFT OF PEACE

Praying the rosary daily is one of the greatest gifts we can give to ourselves, the world, Mary, and Jesus. This profound Marian devotion can promote peace in our hearts and in the world at large. More importantly, it is a means to grow closer to Jesus.

We pray the rosary in Mary's honor because she is the purest role model for discipleship and evangelization. She was the first person to accept Jesus into her life, and she did so eagerly and without hesitation. Mary's goodness and her love for God resulted in the ultimate blessing: to hold the Son of God within her very being. God chose her to carry and raise Jesus, and she cared for and loved him like no one else could.

Mary also is our mother. Jesus gave us his mother at the cross saying to her, "Woman, behold, your son," and then saying to his disciple, John, who represents all humanity, "Behold, your mother" (John 19:26-27). Mary is concerned for the salvation of her children. Throughout history, visionaries who have claimed to have received apparitions (extraordinary appearances) of her have reported that she always requests an increase in prayer. She asks that we turn toward God and away from anything that keeps us from God.

The Rosary Prayer by Prayer

When saying the rosary we repeatedly ask Mary to pray for us. Scripture tells us to request prayers from others, particularly those who are holy. "Pray for one another, that you may be healed. The fervent prayer of a righteous person is very powerful" (James 5:16).

Then who better to request prayers from than Mary? When the Angel Gabriel appeared to her to tell her she would conceive Jesus, Gabriel addressed her as "favored one" (Luke 1:28). The angel told her that the Lord was with her. (See Luke 1:28.) If God is with Mary, and she was entrusted to raise the savior of the world, she certainly can be trusted to carry our prayers to her Son.

When we pray to her, we can be confident that she listens. Anyone with a devotion to Mary will tell you how their prayers have been answered. Our Holy Mother takes our prayers straight to her Son, who denies her nothing. Remember the wedding at Cana? Jesus performed his first public miracle at the request of his mother. (See John 2:1-11.)

The rosary may be Marian in tone but it is God's presence in the world on which we reflect. When we pray the rosary or participate in any other devotion to Mary, it is God alone whom we adore and worship. "To Jesus through Mary" is a common saying. Showing devotion to Mary always leads to a deeper love of and devotion to her Son. We go to Mary in prayer and with her to Jesus.

Consider for a moment the many ways we honor the Trinity with the rosary. Through the prayers and mysteries we declare our fundamental beliefs, ask for God's forgiveness and mercy, give praise, and acknowledge the power of the Holy Spirit. Also we contemplate God's generosity and compassion through the incarnation, life, death, resurrection, and ascension of Jesus. As with all Marian devotion, the rosary is a means to a greater understanding of the Lord. It can assist us with our conversion – our journey to the Lord and away from anything that prevents this journey.

Development of the Rosary

The rosary is a devotion which has evolved over nearly a thousand years into the beautiful blend of prayers and meditations that we know today. The use of objects to help count prayers dates back to 500 B.C. In ancient times stones, dried berries, or beads were tossed from one pile to another to track the number of prayers being said. Prayer ropes later were used by Eastern religions including the Orthodox, Hindu, Buddhist, and Moslem faiths.

Some of the dates and details surrounding the rosary vary from source to source, but it appears that it wasn't until the beginning of the second millennium A.D. that this prayer form took hold in the Christian faith. Around 1096 Irish monks continued a daily practice of reciting the 150 psalms of the Book of Psalms of David, known as the Psalter, as had been done since antiquity. However, this practice proved difficult for the monks.

Many of them were illiterate; therefore they could not read the psalms. Others could read but could not afford to purchase the Psalter. Memorizing the 150 psalms was nearly impossible.

As an alternative the monks began reciting 150 Our Fathers. Given that the Lord's Prayer also was found in Scripture, the monks thought the substitution was

17

acceptable. They kept count of the 150 Our Fathers by following knots or beads tied on a string.

During the Middle Ages prayers were said in Latin. The Our Father was then known as the *Pater Noster*, which is Our Father in Latin. The prayer rope to keep count of the number of prayers became known by the same name.

Not long after that *Ave Marias*, which is Latin for Hail Marys, replaced the Lord's Prayer. The first half of the Hail Mary consists of two verses from Scripture–the greeting by the Angel Gabriel to Mary at the Annunciation and the greeting by Elizabeth to Mary at the Visitation. The second half of the prayer varied until it first appeared in the *Roman Breviary* in 1568.

With the substitution of the Hail Marys the rope became known as the rosary. The word "rosary" comes from the Latin *rosarium,* which means rose garden or grouping of roses in something such as a garland, wreath, or bouquet. In the rosary the Hail Marys are like roses for Mary, our Blessed Mother.

The concept of the mysteries was added possibly as early as the fourteenth century. The Carthusian monasteries are thought to have included little Bible reflections at the end of each Hail Mary. Later these reflections before each decade developed into what we now call mysteries.

Pope Leo X accepted the rosary on behalf of the Church in 1520. Pope Pius V officially approved it as a means of devotion in 1569.

The Rosary and Jesus' Gift of Peace

The Way to Peace

Jesus gave us the gift of peace before his death and resurrection. Jesus said, "Peace I leave with you; my peace I give to you" (John 14:27). He said that this peace is not like the peace we know in this world and that our hearts should not be troubled or afraid.

But human failings can prevent us from realizing this peace. Weaknesses such as jealousy, envy, hatred, prejudice, selfishness, fear, and social injustices obstruct the ability to accept Jesus and his gift of peace. When we are not loving and serving one another, we are not serving the Lord. We are not trusting in Jesus and holding him in the center of our lives. And there can be no peace without Jesus.

Reading Scripture, receiving the Eucharist, and praying the rosary are powerful means to the gift of peace. We can turn to God in prayer to ask for the needed strength, courage, and humility to overcome our weaknesses and reconcile our differences between us and our brothers and sisters, as well as between us and God. We can pray for our continuous conversion so that we may know God's peace.

Only a handful of apparitions of Mary have been approved out of the several hundred that have been investigated by the Catholic Church. (Church approval indicates that the supernatural character of the case cannot be explained, there was no impediment in the visionary, nor was there any fraud or anything of demonic origin. A positive ruling does not require us to believe.)

The apparitions of Mary to three children in Fatima, Portugal in 1917 were very quickly and emphatically

recognized by the Church as "worthy of belief." At
Fatima Mary offered the rosary as a weapon against the
war that was in progress (World War I) and the war that
would follow (World War II). Each time she appeared to
the children she asked that the rosary be prayed every day
for world peace. On October 13, 1917 Mary referred to
herself as the Lady of the Rosary.

Praying the rosary is an effective method of promoting peace in the world because it begins by promoting
peace in our own hearts. The meditative rhythm of the
prayers is very calming. This relaxed state enhances our
ability to reflect on the events in the lives of Jesus and
Mary and engage in an ongoing conversation with them.
The repetition frees the mind of the need for analysis
and activates the imaginative consciousness. This mindful
contemplation allows for a rich religious experience.

While praying the rosary it is often found that answers
to problems will surface. What had been a source of
stress seems somewhat relieved. When we are quiet and
still we can hear God more clearly. It is not unusual to
end the rosary happier and with a renewed level of trust
and faith in God.

So imagine for a moment how the world might be if
each one of us began our day with the rosary. Everyday
would be founded in prayer. Everyday would begin with
communication with Mary and Jesus. Everyday would be
founded on the Word. Everyone would begin everyday in
God's peace. If everyone prayed the rosary everyday, the
world could not be anything other than peaceful.

THE PRAYERS AND MYSTERIES OF THE ROSARY

The rosary is like a bouquet of prayers. Each prayer of this lovely bouquet is a fragrant flower. As we pray, the prayers blossom. Delicate yet vibrant, they emit their fragrance from the heart and out through prayerful hands to Mary and on to our loving God.

The prayers of the rosary include the Our Father, Hail Mary, and Glory Be. It is customary to also include the Apostles' Creed at the beginning and the Hail Holy Queen at the end of the rosary. You will find these prayers with the four rosaries in this book. And like the greenery that ties the flowers together in a bouquet, throughout the rosary we meditate upon events in the life of Jesus, Mary, and the Holy Spirit.

The rosary may be prayed in a number of ways. The traditional manner is known as the Dominican rosary with five, ten, fifteen, or twenty decades (sets of ten Hail Marys). The five decade rosary is the most common. This form includes one set of mysteries for every five decades. Other forms of prayers which use a rosary or a set of beads are called chaplets or coronas.

The section of the rosary from the crucifix to the centerpiece is referred to as the pendant. It consists of the crucifix, a single bead, three beads in row, a single

bead, and then the centerpiece, which looks like a medal.
The centerpiece varies from one rosary to
another. It often is two-sided with Mary on one side and
Jesus on the other. But it can have any design, photo,
words, or representation on it.

The actual rosary is the loop or circle of beads.
This includes chain links, five sets of ten beads (called
a decade), a single bead between the decades, and
the centerpiece.

The Richness of the Prayers

We begin and end the rosary with the Sign of the
Cross. We offer our prayers in the name of God the
Father, Son, and Holy Spirit. In this way we honor
the Trinity.

The first prayer is the Apostles' Creed. It is prayed
while holding the crucifix. The Creed is a declaration of
our basic Christian principals dating to about A.D. 125.
The prayer is believed to be based on fundamental beliefs
outlined by the Apostles at Pentecost. This profession of
faith is thought to have been preached by Saint Peter,
Saint Paul, and their disciples to the Christian community
at Rome.

The next prayer of the rosary, said on the first single
bead, is the Our Father. In addition it is prayed after each
mystery, which is before each decade. The Our Father
also is referred to as the Lord's Prayer. When the disciples
asked Jesus how to pray, Jesus responded with the Our
Father, the perfect prayer. We find the Our Father in
Scripture in Matthew 6:9-13.

In the Our Father we praise God (*Our Father who art in
heaven, hallowed be thy name*). We acknowledge the final

coming of the reign of God *(Thy kingdom come)*. We submit ourselves to God's will *(Thy will be done on earth, as it is in heaven)*. We trust in God to care for our daily needs *(Give us this day our daily bread)*. We ask God to forgive us and promise to forgive those who have hurt us as well *(and forgive us our trespasses, as we forgive those who trespass against us)*. And finally, we ask God to protect us from Satan and any action which hurts God *(and lead us not into temptation, but deliver us from evil. Amen)*.

On the cluster of three beads in the middle of the pendant we say three Hail Marys. Sometimes these Hail Marys are prayed for a special intention, such as for an increase of faith, hope, and charity. Hail Marys also are said on each bead of each decade throughout the main circlet of beads.

The repetition of ten Hail Marys in a row promotes a calm, meditative effect. In this state, our ability to be open to God is enhanced. This is an opportunity for expressing our deepest concerns, listening for direction, and accepting healing. Current medical research is proving that this type of prayerful meditation has many health benefits.

The Hail Mary is comprised of five powerful parts.

1. The first part, *Hail Mary full of grace, the Lord is with thee, blessed art thou amongst women,* comes from the Angel Gabriel's greeting to Mary (Luke 1:28). The salutation recognizes Mary's purity and favor with God, as it is God who greets Mary through the angel. God filled Mary with grace (at her conception) in preparation for bearing the Christ child within her.

2. The second part, *and blessed is the fruit of your womb*, is based on Elizabeth's greeting to Mary (Luke 1:42). Elizabeth and her unborn child, who would become known as John the Baptist, realized the child Mary was carrying was divine. Scripture tells us that when Mary approached Elizabeth, the child inside Elizabeth leaped with joy (Luke 1:44).

3. The third part is simply the name, *Jesus*. Jesus is at the center of the Hail Mary and our hearts.

4. *Holy Mary, Mother of God*, denotes Mary as the *Theotokos*, the God-bearer. At the third Ecumenical Council in Ephesus, in the year 431, it was deemed that Jesus always was God, and therefore, Mary was the Mother of God, the bearer of God.

5. We end the Hail Mary asking Mary to *Pray for us sinners now and at the hour of our death*. We ask Mary for her prayers and to bring us to her Son at the end of this life.

The next prayer of the rosary is the Glory Be. The Glory Be is what is known as a doxology (a short prayer which praises God). All glory at all times belongs to the Trinity (God the Father, God the Son, and God the Holy Spirit). Sometimes the Glory Be is referred to as a lesser doxology. The Gloria said during liturgy is referred to as the greater doxology.

Prayers of praise are found throughout Scripture. In many verses glory is given to the Father forever and ever. An example of this can be found in Galatians 1:4-5.

The Prayers and Mysteries of the Rosary

Giving glory to God the Father, Son, and Holy Spirit became popular in the fourth century. The prayer we say today has been used since the seventh century and is prayed frequently in the Liturgy of the Hours and with a variety of other prayers.

The last prayer of the rosary is the Hail, Holy Queen. Here, again, we honor Mary in prayer. We address her as Queen, Mother of Mercy, our life, our sweetness, and our hope. She is our gracious advocate (supporter). She is the clement (merciful), loving, and sweet Virgin Mary. We end the Hail, Holy Queen with a request for Mary to pray for us.

The prayer is thought to have been written by Hermann Contractus. Bishop Adhemar composed a song based on the Hail, Holy Queen before venturing on a crusade in 1096. Some religious orders sing this prayer daily except on Holy Thursday and Good Friday.

We also may wish to add a prayer of contrition to our rosary in an attempt to make reparation for the occasions we have hurt God, ourselves, or others. In such a prayer we acknowledge the sins we have committed, ask for forgiveness, and promise to do our best not to sin again. This prayer can be a formal prayer such as the Act of Contrition or can be said in our own words.

Meditating on the Mysteries

Throughout the rosary we periodically stop to reflect upon a mystery. This is a key step in tuning into the power of the rosary. Through meditation we contemplate not simply the meaning and impact of the mystery, but of God and God's revelation to us during that particular event and throughout the history of humanity.

The Rosary Prayer by Prayer

Traditionally, meditation is a practice that begins by quieting the body and the mind and breathing deeply and slowly. When we meditate we reflect upon something; we study, or ponder it. When we meditate upon the mysteries of the rosary we reflect upon them intellectually and emotionally. We take them into our body, mind, and soul, not only thinking about them but feeling them.

The mysteries are an integral element in the fullness of the rosary and richness of devotion prompted by this prayer tool. Mysteries are Scriptural or Traditional reflections on the events in the lives of Jesus and Mary. They tell the story of redemption, making the rosary a prayer of the entire history of salvation.

God speaks to us through Scripture in new ways every time we hear the Word. Have you noticed how the same Biblical passage may be the answer to one question you may have at one time and also answer an entirely different question another time? You will find this to be true of the mysteries of the rosary also, because they are rooted in the Bible.

When I was a child the Joyful Mysteries were my favorite. But I understood these mysteries differently when I was a young mother, and in yet another way now that I am a mature woman. The words are unchanged, but as my life changes I find new meaning in them.

As a child every time I prayed the rosary with the Joyful Mysteries, it was like Christmas. The anticipation of the coming of the Baby Jesus would mount with the Annunciation–Angel Gabriel's message to Mary that she would be the mother of Jesus; and then the Visitation–Mary's visit to her cousin, Elizabeth, and the reaction of the unborn John the Baptist in his mother's womb when

Jesus was in his presence; and finally, the birth of the Infant Jesus, the Christ, the Anointed One.

I also loved to ponder the Presentation–Baby Jesus being carried into the Temple by his parents to be dedicated to the Lord. Then I would reflect on the finding of the twelve year-old Jesus in the Temple. I would imagine Jesus, as a child like me, and yet so different, in the Temple with the teachers discussing theological topics.

When my children were little and I prayed the rosary with the Joyful Mysteries, I thought more about Mary as the mother of Jesus. I looked to her as a role model for motherhood. I would wonder what Mary would do in certain parental situations I encountered and how I could be the God-loving mother that she was.

At this point in my life the Joyful Mysteries are helping me to realize the great love God has for creation. I am humbled by the Incarnation, God's sacrifice and salvation. I am in awe of how God was revealed in the human person of Jesus.

Reflecting on the mysteries can be as inspiring and revealing as reflecting on the Word, because with every mystery we are reflecting on the Lord. When we ponder upon the meaning of a Bible passage the journey takes us to an endless amount of places and levels. We begin to understand things a little more fully. We become closer to God and love Jesus more by thinking about these great mysteries.

Reflection on the mysteries must begin with the Scriptural verses to which the event relates. Look closely at the words as they describe what is happening. Imagine how it would feel to have been there in that place and time, to have witnessed that particular miraculous event–to have felt, touched, and smelled the glory of God in that extraordinary moment.

You also may contemplate how this event relates to other biblical stories. Some passages reflect teachings of the Hebrew Scriptures (the Old Testament). Others foreshadow events to come in the New Testament.

For example, by reflecting on Abraham (Gen 15:2-6) and Rachel's (Gen 30:1) desperate cries for a child we understand the significance of Elizabeth's pregnancy (Luke 1:36-37). In ancient times, to be childless was equated with being unloved by God, because children are a blessing from God. When Elizabeth became pregnant in her advanced age her status in the community was raised as did her personal joy and gratitude.

Once you have spent some time meditating on the Scriptural aspects of the mysteries consider the teachings of the Church in relation to this event. What does the *Catechism of the Catholic Church* say about it? How do Church documents respond to it? What beliefs do we have from our rich Tradition in regards to this event?

You may meditate upon the significance of the event and ask some questions such as: Why might the event have happened in that way? What can be learned from it? How does it affect our humanity? How should it affect your every thought, word, and action?

In addition the mystery can be looked at from a cultural point of view. How do the social or natural sciences add insight to the reflection? How does this mystery relate to social justice? Does this mystery bring you to a higher level of personal ethics?

The mystery also can be meditated upon from a personal point of view. How would you respond if God asked you to perform a similar mission? How have you seen others respond to such a call?

For example when meditating upon the birth of Christ, you might reflect upon the meaning of your own birth. You also may ask yourself how you will help someone "to be born" or "give birth" to a new way of being. You may think about how you can be more Christ-like, or how you can follow the examples of Mary and Jesus and live as they lived.

Of course time will not allow you to contemplate all of these questions for every reflection of every mystery every time you pray the rosary. These questions are offered as suggestions. Some days you may wish to focus on one aspect, such as how it would feel to have witnessed the event firsthand. Another day you may wish to think about how you can live the message of the event more fully.

You may wish to focus on a particular mystery for an entire day or even a liturgical season. Perhaps the only quiet time you have in a day is the ten minutes you spend walking home after putting your children on the school bus. You may choose to pray one decade of the rosary and spend an Advent season contemplating the Annunciation or the Lenten season reflecting upon the Crowing with Thorns during those few free minutes each day.

From the sixteenth century until 2002 we had only three sets of mysteries. These mysteries were the Joyful, Sorrowful, and Glorious Mysteries. In October of 2002 Pope John Paul II proposed a fourth set of mysteries, called the Luminous Mysteries. Also known as the Mysteries of Light, these events add greatly to a more complete reflection.

The Rosary Prayer by Prayer

The Joyful Mysteries focus on the Incarnation and early life of Jesus. They encompass the events prior to the conception of the fully divine and fully human Jesus to Jesus' twelfth year. These mysteries include the Annunciation, Visitation, Nativity, Presentation, and Finding in the Temple.

The Luminous Mysteries focus on the public life of Jesus. They highlight Jesus' ministry and example of true discipleship. The Luminous mysteries are the Baptism of Jesus in the River Jordan, Jesus' First Public Miracle at the Wedding in Cana, Jesus' Proclamation of the Coming of the Kingdom, the Transfiguration of the Lord, and the Institution of the Eucharist.

The Sorrowful Mysteries concentrate on the Passion of Christ. Through these mysteries we acknowledge the suffering and death that Jesus endured for our salvation. They are mournful yet incredibly heartwarming and loving. The Sorrowful Mysteries include the Agony in the Garden, Scourging at the Pillar, Crowning with Thorns, Carrying of the Cross, and Crucifixion.

The Glorious Mysteries contain some of the greatest wonders of our beliefs and Tradition. They are hopeful and truly magnificent. These mysteries honor Jesus, the Holy Spirit, and the Virgin Mary. The Glorious Mysteries are the Resurrection and Ascension of Jesus, the Descent of the Holy Spirit, and the Assumption and Coronation of Mary.

The current suggestion is that the Glorious Mysteries are reflected upon on Sundays and Wednesdays; the Joyful Mysteries on Mondays and Saturdays, the Sorrowful Mysteries on Tuesdays and Fridays, and the Luminous Mysteries on Thursdays. However, any set of mysteries may be said on any day.

The Prayers and Mysteries of the Rosary

The Intentions of Our Prayers

The rosary may be prayed for many reasons. You may
wish to say the rosary simply to be with Mary and Jesus,
or you may pray for a special intention. Intentions may be
stated at any time during the rosary. The entire rosary may
be offered for a particular intention, or a request may be
made before each decade. Sometimes when I pray, I think
of a friend, family member, or acquaintance before each
Hail Mary.

The three main categories of prayer intentions are
adoration, petition, and thanksgiving. Prayers of adoration acknowledge the greatness of God. We worship
God, not for God's benefit, but to strengthen our own
faith. When we praise the Lord we recognize the wonder
of creation and God's glory shining through all things at
all times.

Prayers of petition encompass all that is asked of God
from the request for a winning baseball game to the
healing of a terminally ill loved one. We may bring our
prayers to God with confidence. Nothing is too small or
impossible to lay before the Lord.

And never to be omitted, prayers of thanksgiving
show gratitude for the endless daily blessings we receive.
Our God is loving and generous however, God answers
all prayers in God's way and time. We can end every
prayer in gratitude for God loves us and listens to our
prayers. The only prayer unanswered is the one that
isn't asked.

The Rosary Prayer by Prayer

PRAYING THE ROSARY WITH THIS BOOK

Rosary beads offer an easy way to pray. As you move from bead to bead you embark on a pilgrimage. With each prayer you take a step closer to Jesus. The pathway is laid out for you. You only need to follow along.

The intention of this book is to assist you on that journey and promote a richer rosary prayer experience. The book can be used to teach the novice how to pray the rosary. It can be used by the intermediate who would like a better understanding of the mysteries. The book also can be used as an aid in meditation by those who are experienced at saying the rosary.

The word "rosary" refers to a specific series of prayers along with one of the accompanying four sets of mysteries. The word also refers to the prayer rope or circlet of beads with the decade pattern. When we pray the rosary we are reciting prayers in a certain order and, most often, using rosary beads. In its true form the rosary is not read. It is said, prayed, or recited.

Repeatedly in my years of teaching the rosary, I have encountered people who want to pray the rosary but are overwhelmed by just how to recite it. Instruction pamphlets can be confusing. There seems to be so much to remember. But you really don't have to remember very much when praying on the beads. The beads cue you as to what to pray and when to reflect on the mysteries.

Some people have told me that they have said the rosary all of their lives, but without the mysteries. Others have said that they recite the title of the mystery, but they do not stop to reflect upon it. The mysteries are an integral element in this beautiful form of prayer and absolutely must be included. This is the essence of praying the rosary.

An acceptable option is to substitute the mysteries with another Scriptural reading. You may wish to choose one of the psalms or a chapter from a book of the Bible and read a verse from that psalm or chapter before each decade of the rosary. Using the rosary like this is a wonderful way of reflecting upon Scripture.

Your interest in reading this book suggests your desire to know more about the rosary. The fact that people have prayed it for nearly 500 years indicates it is a valuable prayer. Please do give it a chance if it is not already a part of your daily routine. With a little practice you will find that the rosary is a marvelous method of communicating with God.

The Rosary Pages

The following chapters of this book contain the prayers for four entire rosaries with the mysteries. You will find one complete rosary with the Joyful Mysteries, one with the Luminous Mysteries, one with the Sorrowful Mysteries, and one with the Glorious Mysteries. The prayers are in the order in which they are prayed.

Praying the Rosary with this Book

Simply choose the rosary with the mysteries you would like to pray and follow along prayer by prayer, page by page, to pray that rosary.

The words of the prayers are updated a bit from those I have used throughout my life. If you look at other publications you will find slight variations in the words of the prayers. This is because an attempt has been made to modernize the language and make the words more inclusive. For example the word "you" may be substituted for "thou" as in "blessed art thou among women." When praying remember that the prayers are yours, so please say them in a way that is most meaningful to you.

The next chapters contain the prayer to be said on the left side of each page. On the right side you will find a scan (a type of photocopy) of an actual rosary with the corresponding beads circled. For example, if you are reading or reciting the Our Father before the second decade, you will see that bead circled. For those who are new to the rosary, once you have prayed this two-dimensional rosary, you will find it much easier to use the beads on your own.

When praying the Hail Marys in a decade the entire decade is circled. You can keep track of praying the ten Hail Marys by pointing to each bead on the paper, praying on your fingers, or using your own rosary beads.

You will see on the rosary scans that I begin the decades on the left side of the centerpiece. I started from the left because it is easier to follow visually. But it doesn't matter which direction you take. You may pray from the left or right, whichever way is most comfortable for you.

The Rosary Prayer by Prayer

Typically when meditating upon the mysteries, the title is announced and a few moments are taken to contemplate its meaning. For example when approaching the third Sorrowful Mystery one would say, "The Crowning with Thorns," and then stop and think about what that means in relation to the Scriptures.

In this book you will find a page of Scripture, a reflection, and an illustration for each mystery. The Scripture you will encounter is either an account of the mystery to which it refers or is related to that event in some way. In addition after some of the Scriptural passages I've included suggestions for other passages you may find of interest that relate to that event. Although, I remind you once again that you may read any verse from the Bible with any mystery.

The reflection included with each mystery should offer some insight or a new perspective to your prayer. You may find when reading these pages your mind will wonder to your own reflection. This also may happen when reflecting on the illustrations. These pages are included to trigger your own thoughts so that you may ponder the mysteries in your own way and have a conversation with God that is as unique as you are.

Joseph Cannella's illustrations offer some unusual perspectives. They are not the typical representation of the great mysteries. For example, The Visitation illustration shows Elizabeth listening to Jesus in Mary's womb, the Agony in the Garden offers a close-up of a modern looking Jesus, and the Assumption is seen in a reflection in a body of water as rain falls from the heavens. Be sure to read the section on the reflection page that describes the accompanying illustration for insight into what Mr. Cannella is zeroing in on, and look closely for symbols not noticed at first glance (such as doves in Mary's eyes in the Annunciation).

Also please be sure to look at the back of this book for important resources. There you will find some other prayers which are sometimes said after or with the rosary. In addition you will find an appendix with a typical instruction on saying the rosary as pointed out on a scan of the rosary (The Map of the Rosary). A list of some Marian organizations which may be of interest to you also is included.

Styles of Rosary Beads

Rosary beads come in every color and can be made from any material. Most commonly you will find them made of plastic, glass, crystal, wood, metal, seeds, or stones. They range in price from inexpensive to very expensive. Select a rosary that appeals to you in color and content and that feels good in your hands.

I have distributed hundreds of rosaries and am fascinated by who selects which rosary. Some people like bright colors. Others want something subtle. Some like large beads. Others like the feel of teeny, tiny little beads between their fingers. Even the texture of the bead can be important to you personally.

The number of rosaries one owns also varies. Some people prefer always to pray on the same rosary. Others have several different kinds. My father only would use the rosary on which my mother taught him when they were newlyweds. He died with this rosary in his hands.

I myself have many rosaries. Each one is special to me. I have a rosary from my grandmother and one from my mother. I have rosaries from the Marian shrines at Fatima, Medjugorje, and Knock. I also have two from Rome; one of which was given to me by my daughter, Erin, and the other from the priest who baptized me. In addition I have one that was made for me from the seed "Job's Tears."

Rosary beads can be found or ordered from most Catholic gift shops. The names and contact information for sources for rosaries are also in the back of this book.

Praying Alone or With Others

The rosary most often is prayed individually, but there are several other options. I enjoy the rosary said in private and in groups. Both are wonderful in different ways.

Due to chronic illness, I feel best in the morning if I rise slowly. I set my alarm clock at least a half an hour earlier than needed. I then sit up in bed and pray the rosary. This practice allows me the opportunity to begin my day focused on God.

When I pray the rosary alone I like to concentrate on the mysteries for a longer period of time than what is commonly done as a group. Sometimes I also like to think about the people in my life, saying their names one by one, before each Hail Mary.

However, I also enjoy praying aloud in a community because then all of our prayers rumble through the room. It is as if each of our intentions are multiplied by every person praying, which is a powerful thought. In addition, there is a closeness that people often feel when praying the rosary together.

Praying the Rosary with this Book

The group of people with whom you pray may be members of the same church, a circle of friends, or family. When I was a child my family prayed the rosary together during Lent. We knelt around my parents bed under a massive crucifix that hung on the wall above it. Anytime the family prays together, it is bonded in faith and love.

You will notice that when the rosary is prayed with other people one person typically acts as a leader. The leader recites the first half of the prayers. The rest of the group responds with the second half. The leader also announces the mysteries.

The leader may wish to read a corresponding passage from the Bible for each mystery. A short song also may be sung after each reflection. Another possibility is to have five or six people take turns leading a section or decade rather than one leader. Or if the group is very large, each person can say one prayer.

Another option to consider is to pray the rosary along with an audio tape or CD. Some of these recordings are inspiring and have Marian hymns after the prayers. One of my favorites is produced by the Sisters of St. Paul. The sisters sing like angels at the end of each set of mysteries.

The rosary also can be prayed along with programs on television. Channel EWTN runs tapings of the rosary throughout the day. They have a beautiful recording from Jerusalem that highlights the locations where the mysteries actually took place. It is quite moving to see where Jesus carried his cross and then meditate upon the mystery.

The Gift of the Rosary

I do hope this book will make praying the complete rosary very clear. Once you commit to praying it daily, you will find the need to continue to do so. It is my staying power and a gift I give to myself, Mary, and Jesus. My day begins calmly and happily. I find myself thinking about the mysteries throughout the day and looking at everything a little differently because of them.

And since saying the rosary has been such an integral part of my daily life most of my life, my troubles are eased simply by fingering the beads. When I am sad, worried or nervous I reach for my rosary and am quickly reminded of God's presence.

If you do not have the time to pray the entire set of mysteries, try praying one decade periodically throughout the day or at least one decade each day. When using this book you may select a page of Scripture, read the reflection and then pray one Our Father, ten Hail Marys, and a Glory Be. You may feel that this allows you the opportunity to reflect more deeply on that mystery.

My wish for you is that you find the comfort and inspiration that I have found in the beautiful prayers and meditations of the rosary. May you grow in love for Jesus and Mary, and may the rosary assist you with your continuous conversion, your journey toward God. In Jesus' name, I wish you peace and joy. Amen.

Praying the Rosary with this Book

The Rosary Prayer by Prayer

PART II

THE ROSARY WITH

THE MYSTERIES

The Rosary Prayer by Prayer

THE ROSARY

WITH THE

JOYFUL

MYSTERIES

SIGN OF THE CROSS

In the name of the Father,
and of the Son,
and of the Holy Spirit.
Amen.

THE APOSTLES' CREED

I believe in God, the Father Almighty,
Creator of heaven and earth; and in
Jesus Christ, His only son, Our Lord,
who was conceived by the Holy Spirit,
born of the Virgin Mary, suffered
under Pontius Pilate, was crucified,
died, and was buried. He descended
into hell; the third day He arose again
from the dead; He ascended into
heaven and sits at the right hand of
God, the Father Almighty; from
thence He shall come to judge the
living and the dead. I believe in the
Holy Spirit, the Holy Catholic church,
the communion of saints, the forgiveness of sins, the resurrection of the
body and life everlasting. Amen.

OUR FATHER

Our Father, Who art in Heaven,
Hallowed be Thy name; Thy kingdom
come; Thy will be done on earth as it
is in heaven. Give us this day our daily
bread; and forgive us our trespasses as
we forgive those who trespass against
us; and lead us not into temptation,
but deliver us from evil. Amen

HAIL MARY

Hail Mary, full of grace, the Lord is with you; blessed are you among women and blessed is the fruit of your womb, Jesus. Holy Mary, mother of God, pray for us sinners, now and at the hour of our death. Amen.

HAIL MARY

Hail Mary, full of grace, the Lord is with you; blessed are you among women and blessed is the fruit of your womb, Jesus. Holy Mary, mother of God, pray for us sinners, now and at the hour of our death. Amen.

HAIL MARY

Hail Mary, full of grace, the Lord is with you; blessed are you among women and blessed is the fruit of your womb, Jesus. Holy Mary, mother of God, pray for us sinners, now and at the hour of our death. Amen.

GLORY BE

Glory be to the Father, and to the
Son, and to the Holy Spirit, as it was
in the beginning, is now, and ever shall
be, world without end. Amen.

FIRST JOYFUL MYSTERY
THE ANNUNCIATION

And coming to her, he said, "Hail, favored one! The Lord is with you." But she was greatly troubled at what was said and pondered what sort of greeting this might be. Then the angel said to her, "Do not be afraid, Mary, for you have found favor with God. Behold, you will conceive in your womb and bear a son, and you shall name him Jesus. He will be great and will be called Son of the Most High, and the Lord God will give him the throne of David his father, and he will rule over the house of Jacob forever, and of his kingdom there will be no end." But Mary said to the angel, "How can this be, since I have no relations with a man?" And the angel said to her in reply, "The holy Spirit will come upon you, and the power of the Most High will over-shadow you. Therefore the child to be born will be called holy, the Son of God. And behold, Elizabeth, your relative, has also conceived a son in her old age, and this is the sixth month for her who was called barren; for nothing will be impossible for God" (Luke 1:28-37).

REFLECTION ON THE ANNUNCIATION

Mary didn't hesitate to agree to God's request. The young teenager accepted the responsibility for carrying and raising a child that guaranteed the salvation of the people of her time and all future generations. The guidance, education, and childhood safety of the Anointed One was in her hands.

Mary knew that she had everything necessary for her role in God's plan. She trusted in God's vocation for her and that God would be with her every step of the way.

Mary conceived a child and yet remained a virgin. Elizabeth conceived a child at an age thought to be beyond childbearing. These two events proved once again that nothing is impossible with God.

When God calls upon us we are allowed the choice to refuse or accept the mission. If you were Mary, how would you have responded?

Jesus' cry is heard in the neglected child, the hungry single mother, the ailing cancer patient, the lonely widower, and the forgotten veteran in a military hospital. How do you respond to God's call by responding to people in need of food, shelter, companionships, or guidance? How do you welcome Jesus into your life?

ANNUNCIATION PRAYER

Lord, grant me the courage to accept your mission for me and the strength to accomplish it with the dignity, grace, and holiness of Mary.

ANNUNCIATION ILLUSTRATION

Mary takes God's plan into her heart.

OUR FATHER

Our Father, Who art in Heaven, Hallowed be Thy name; Thy kingdom come; Thy will be done on earth as it is in heaven. Give us this day our daily bread; and forgive us our trespasses as we forgive those who trespass against us; and lead us not into temptation, but deliver us from evil. Amen.

First Decade: Pray one Hail Mary on each bead of the first decade for a total of ten Hail Marys.

HAIL MARY

Hail Mary, full of grace, the Lord is with you; blessed are you among women and blessed is the fruit of your womb, Jesus. Holy Mary, mother of God, pray for us sinners, now and at the hour of our death. Amen.

GLORY BE

Glory be to the Father, and to the
Son, and to the Holy Spirit, as it was
in the beginning, is now, and ever shall
be, world without end. Amen.

SECOND JOYFUL MYSTERY
THE VISITATION

During those days Mary set out and traveled to the hill country in haste to a town of Judah, where she entered the house of Zechariah and greeted Elizabeth. When Elizabeth heard Mary's greeting, the infant leaped in her womb, and Elizabeth, filled with the holy Spirit, cried out in a loud voice and said, "Most blessed are you among women, and blessed is the fruit of your womb. And how does this happen to me, that the mother of my Lord should come to me? For at the moment the sound of your greeting reached my ears, the infant in my womb leaped for joy. Blessed are you who believed that what was spoken to you by the Lord would be fulfilled."

And Mary said:/"My soul proclaims the greatness of the Lord;/my spirit rejoices in God my savior./For he has looked upon his handmaid's lowliness; /behold, from now on will all ages call me blessed./The Mighty One has done great things for me,/ and holy is his name" (Luke 1:39-49).

REFLECTION ON THE VISITATION

When Mary heard from the Angel Gabriel of her
cousin's pregnancy, she immediately took the long journey
to see her. Mary may have felt nauseous or fatigued,
which is typical in early pregnancy, but she did not think
of her own needs. Even before he was born, Mary
brought Jesus to the house of Zechariah. She brought
Jesus to the people.

The two women had much to celebrate. Imagine their
unbounded joy. Not only were they pregnant, they were
expecting sons that would change the course of history.

Elizabeth's baby was filled with the Holy Spirit. Her
child would grow up to become an important prophet.
The pregnancy also ended the stigma associated with
being childless.

Mary was carrying the Son of God. She could feel the
Messiah moving and growing within her. At no time
could any human being be physically closer to Jesus than
Mary was at that moment.

If you were with the cousins during their three months
together how would you have cared for the women? How
do you care for the mothers-to-be and the unborn in your
community? How do you bring Jesus to your friends and
family?

VISITATION PRAYER

May the angels guide me toward those in need of
compassion, generosity, and the Word.

VISITATION ILLUSTRATION

Elizabeth listens to the unborn Jesus in Mary's womb.

OUR FATHER

Our Father, Who art in Heaven,
Hallowed be Thy name; Thy kingdom
come; Thy will be done on earth as it
is in heaven. Give us this day our daily
bread; and forgive us our trespasses as
we forgive those who trespass against
us; and lead us not into temptation,
but deliver us from evil. Amen.

Second Decade: Pray one Hail Mary on each bead of the second decade for a total of ten Hail Marys.

HAIL MARY

Hail Mary, full of grace, the Lord is with you; blessed are you among women and blessed is the fruit of your womb, Jesus. Holy Mary, mother of God, pray for us sinners, now and at the hour of our death. Amen.

GLORY BE

Glory be to the Father, and to the
Son, and to the Holy Spirit, as it was
in the beginning, is now, and ever shall
be, world without end. Amen.

THIRD JOYFUL MYSTERY
THE NATIVITY

And Joseph too went up from Galilee from the town of Nazareth to Judea, to the city of David that is called Bethlehem, because he was of the house and family of David, to be enrolled with Mary, his betrothed, who was with child. While they were there, the time came for her to have her child, and she gave birth to her firstborn son. She wrapped him in swaddling clothes and laid him in a manger, because there was no room for them in the inn.

Now there were shepherds in that region living in the fields and keeping the night watch over their flock. The angel of the Lord appeared to them and the glory of the Lord shone around them, and they were struck with great fear. The angel said to them, "Do not be afraid; for behold, I proclaim to you good news of great joy that will be for all the people. For today in the city of David a savior has been born for you who is Messiah and Lord. And this will be a sign for you; you will find an infant wrapped in swaddling clothes and lying in a manger" (Luke 2:4-12).

REFLECTION ON THE NATIVITY

Required by Emperor Augustus to register, Joseph and the very pregnant Mary journeyed from the meager comforts of their home in Nazareth to an overcrowded and unwelcoming city of Bethlehem. Not one person opened their door to the coming of the Messiah. Mary found herself giving birth in a stable, among the field animals, and laying her precious infant in a bed of hay.

The mystery of Jesus' nativity offers much to ponder. God chose to be born in the human form of Jesus in a modest and humble way. There was no cradle, royal robe, servants, or castle awaiting the birth of this King of Kings. Even the very basics were lacking. The most important being to walk this earth entered this world in the most unpretentious, poorest, and dirtiest locations and at quite an inconvenient time for his mother.

When wondering where, how, when, and with whom we find God, we can look to this mystery for some of the answers. Be alert and look around you. Jesus may be found in unexpected times and places.

To whom do you open your door and your heart? How do you prepare for the second coming of Christ?

NATIVITY PRAYER
At all times, in all places, through all people I welcome you into my life, dear Jesus.

NATIVITY ILLUSTRATION
The light of the world lives among us.

OUR FATHER

Our Father, Who art in Heaven,
Hallowed be Thy name; Thy kingdom
come; Thy will be done on earth as it
is in heaven. Give us this day our daily
bread; and forgive us our trespasses as
we forgive those who trespass against
us; and lead us not into temptation,
but deliver us from evil. Amen.

Third Decade: Pray one Hail Mary on each bead of the third decade for a total of ten Hail Marys.

HAIL MARY

Hail Mary, full of grace, the Lord is with you; blessed are you among women and blessed is the fruit of your womb, Jesus. Holy Mary, mother of God, pray for us sinners, now and at the hour of our death. Amen.

GLORY BE

Glory be to the Father, and to the
Son, and to the Holy Spirit, as it was
in the beginning, is now, and ever shall
be, world without end. Amen.

FOURTH JOYFUL MYSTERY
THE PRESENTATION

When the days were completed for their purification according to the law of Moses, they took him up to Jerusalem to present him to the Lord, just as it is written in the law of the Lord, "Every male that opens the womb shall be consecrated to the Lord," and to offer the sacrifice of "a pair of turtledoves or two young pigeons," in accordance with the dictate in the law of the Lord.

Now there was a man in Jerusalem whose name was Simeon. This man was righteous and devout, awaiting the consolation of Israel, and the holy Spirit was upon him. It had been revealed to him by the holy Spirit that he should not see death before he had seen the Messiah of the Lord. He came in the Spirit into the temple; and when the parents brought in the child Jesus to perform the custom of the law in regard to him, he took him into his arms and blessed God, saying:/ "Now, Master, you may let your servant go/in peace, according to your word,/for my eyes have seen your salvation" (Luke 2:22-30).

REFLECTION ON THE PRESENTATION

Mary and Joseph were faithful to the Hebrew Laws. They performed their religious duty after the birth of Jesus by going to Jerusalem for purification, to offer a sacrifice, and present Jesus to the Lord. They went to humbly honor God.

When the family encountered the righteous Simeon in the temple, the man took their baby into his arms. Immediately Simeon recognized the child as the savior and the light of the world. He praised God. Scripture continues saying that Simeon then forewarned the parents of what was to come. (See Luke 2:34-35.)

Simeon knew that the sacrifice the parents brought to the temple was so much more than two birds. One day Mary would endure the greatest pain any mother could experience. She would witness the torture and murder of her cherished child.

How do you follow the duties of your faith? How do you honor the Lord? What gifts have you been given? What gifts do you present to the Lord?

PRESENTATION PRAYER

All that I am and all that I have I dedicate to you Almighty Father, as everything comes from you.

PRESENTATION ILLUSTRATION

Mary presents the infant Jesus to the Lord under the shadow of the cross.

OUR FATHER

Our Father, Who art in Heaven,
Hallowed be Thy name; Thy kingdom
come; Thy will be done on earth as it
is in heaven. Give us this day our daily
bread; and forgive us our trespasses as
we forgive those who trespass against
us; and lead us not into temptation,
but deliver us from evil. Amen.

Fourth Decade: Pray one Hail Mary on each bead of the fourth decade for a total of ten Hail Marys.

HAIL MARY

Hail Mary, full of grace, the Lord is with you; blessed are you among women and blessed is the fruit of your womb, Jesus. Holy Mary, mother of God, pray for us sinners, now and at the hour of our death. Amen.

GLORY BE

Glory be to the Father, and to the
Son, and to the Holy Spirit, as it was
in the beginning, is now, and ever shall
be, world without end. Amen.

FIFTH JOYFUL MYSTERY
THE FINDING IN THE
TEMPLE

Each year his parents went to
Jerusalem for the feast of Passover,
and when he was twelve years old,
they went up according to festival
custom. After they had completed its
days, as they were returning, the boy
Jesus remained behind in Jerusalem,
but his parents did not know it.
Thinking that he was in the caravan,
they journeyed for a day and looked
for him among their relatives and
acquaintances, but not finding him,
they returned to Jerusalem to look for
him. After three days they found him
in the temple, sitting in the midst of
the teachers, listening to them and
asking them questions, and all who
heard him were astounded at his
understanding and his answers. When
his parents saw him, they were aston-
ished, and his mother said to him.
"Son, why have you done this to us?
Your father and I have been looking
for you with great anxiety." And he
said to them, "Why were you looking
for me? Did you not know that I must
be in my Father's house?" But they did
not understand what he said to them
(Luke 2:41-50).

REFLECTION ON
THE FINDING IN THE TEMPLE

We don't know by the reading if Jesus intentionally remained in Jerusalem when his family left the city. What we do realize is that at a young age Jesus had a good sense of his purpose. When his parents found him, Jesus was engaged in a mature discussion with the teachers in "his Father's" house.

Jesus was twelve years old when this event occurred. The preteen years begin the transition between childhood and adulthood. A boy naturally pulls away from his parents and begins to find himself at this age.

It is interesting to note that Mary contemplated upon the meaning of the signs she was given that Jesus was not an ordinary child. The Gospel of Luke says that Mary pondered the angel Gabriel's greeting to her at the Annunciation (1:29), reflected on what the shepherds were telling everyone at the Nativity (2:19), was amazed at what Simeon said about Jesus at the Presentation (2:33), and kept everything in her heart after finding Jesus in the temple (2:51). Perhaps this contemplation was Mary's preparation for her role as disciple and mother of the redeemer.

How are you preparing for discipleship? Where do you find Jesus? Where do you find yourself?

FINDING IN THE TEMPLE PRAYER
Jesus I pray for the grace to never lose sight of you.

FINDING IN THE TEMPLE ILLUSTRATION
Mary anxiously searches for her son while Jesus is with the teachers in the temple.

OUR FATHER

Our Father, Who art in Heaven,
Hallowed be Thy name; Thy kingdom
come; Thy will be done on earth as it
is in heaven. Give us this day our daily
bread; and forgive us our trespasses as
we forgive those who trespass against
us; and lead us not into temptation,
but deliver us from evil. Amen.

Fifth Decade: Pray one Hail Mary on each bead of the fifth decade for a total of ten Hail Marys.

HAIL MARY

Hail Mary, full of grace, the Lord is with you; blessed are you among women and blessed is the fruit of your womb, Jesus. Holy Mary, mother of God, pray for us sinners, now and at the hour of our death. Amen.

GLORY BE

Glory be to the Father, and to the
Son, and to the Holy Spirit, as it was
in the beginning, is now, and ever shall
be, world without end. Amen.

HAIL, HOLY QUEEN

Hail, holy Queen, Mother of mercy;
our life, our sweetness and our hope.
To you do we cry, poor banished
children of Eve. To you do we send
up our sighs, mourning and weeping
in this valley of tears. Turn then, most
gracious Advocate, your eyes of
mercy toward us, and after this our
exile, show unto us the blessed fruit
of your womb, Jesus. O clement, O
loving, O sweet Virgin Mary.

V: Pray for us, O holy Mother of
God.

R: That we may become worthy of
the promises of Christ. Amen.

SIGN OF THE CROSS

In the name of the Father,
and of the Son,
and of the Holy Spirit.
Amen.

THE ROSARY

WITH THE

LUMINOUS

MYSTERIES

SIGN OF THE CROSS

In the name of the Father,
and of the Son,
and of the Holy Spirit.
Amen.

THE APOSTLES' CREED

I believe in God, the Father Almighty, Creator of heaven and earth; and in Jesus Christ, His only son, Our Lord, who was conceived by the Holy Spirit, born of the Virgin Mary, suffered under Pontius Pilate, was crucified, died, and was buried. He descended into hell; the third day He arose again from the dead; He ascended into heaven and sits at the right hand of God, the Father Almighty; from thence He shall come to judge the living and the dead. I believe in the Holy Spirit, the Holy Catholic church, the communion of saints, the forgiveness of sins, the resurrection of the body and life everlasting. Amen.

OUR FATHER

Our Father, Who art in Heaven, Hallowed be Thy name; Thy kingdom come; Thy will be done on earth as it is in heaven. Give us this day our daily bread; and forgive us our trespasses as we forgive those who trespass against us; and lead us not into temptation, but deliver us from evil. Amen

HAIL MARY

Hail Mary, full of grace, the Lord is with you; blessed are you among women and blessed is the fruit of your womb, Jesus. Holy Mary, mother of God, pray for us sinners, now and at the hour of our death. Amen.

HAIL MARY

Hail Mary, full of grace, the Lord is with you; blessed are you among women and blessed is the fruit of your womb, Jesus. Holy Mary, mother of God, pray for us sinners, now and at the hour of our death. Amen.

HAIL MARY

Hail Mary, full of grace, the Lord is with you; blessed are you among women and blessed is the fruit of your womb, Jesus. Holy Mary, mother of God, pray for us sinners, now and at the hour of our death. Amen.

GLORY BE

Glory be to the Father, and to the
Son, and to the Holy Spirit, as it was
in the beginning, is now, and ever shall
be, world without end. Amen.

FIRST LUMINOUS MYSTERY
THE BAPTISM OF JESUS

Then Jesus came from Galilee to John at the Jordan to be baptized by him. John tried to prevent him, saying, "I need to be baptized by you, and yet you are coming to me?" Jesus said to him in reply, "Allow it now, for thus it is fitting for us to fulfill all righteousness." Then he allowed him. After Jesus was baptized, he came up from the water and behold, the heavens were opened [for him], and he saw the Spirit of God descending like a dove [and] coming upon him. And a voice came from the heavens, saying, "This is my beloved Son, with whom I am well pleased" (Matt 3:13-17).

Also see: Mark 1:9-11, Luke 3:21-22, John 1:29-34.

REFLECTION ON THE BAPTISM OF JESUS

The humble John prepared the way for Jesus by baptizing people in the Jordan River. John's baptism was a ritual of repentance for the forgiveness of sins. His ministry fulfilled the prophecy given to his father, Zechariah, by an angel that his son would prepare a people fit for the Lord (Luke 1:17).

Jesus asked John to baptize him, but Jesus was without sin. He had no need of baptism or forgiveness. He wanted to be baptized as a model of faith in solidarity with all humankind.

The baptism becomes one of the most remarkable events when all three Persons of the Trinity are revealed together. As God the Son comes out of the water, God the Holy Spirit descends upon him like a dove, and God the Father speaks, claiming Jesus as God's beloved Son. This event is indicative that something monumental is about to happen.

If you were baptized you also were baptized with the Holy Spirit. What do you know about your own baptism? How do you allow the Spirit to work within you? How do you prepare the way for the Lord?

BAPTISM OF JESUS PRAYER

Holy Spirit, guide me to live a life of repentance, love, and compassion as Jesus showed me.

BAPTISM OF JESUS ILLUSTRATION

The Spirit of God descends like a dove upon Jesus.

OUR FATHER

Our Father, Who art in Heaven,
Hallowed be Thy name; Thy kingdom
come; Thy will be done on earth as it
is in heaven. Give us this day our daily
bread; and forgive us our trespasses as
we forgive those who trespass against
us; and lead us not into temptation,
but deliver us from evil. Amen.

First Decade: Pray one Hail Mary on each bead of the first decade for a total of ten Hail Marys.

HAIL MARY

Hail Mary, full of grace, the Lord is with you; blessed are you among women and blessed is the fruit of your womb, Jesus. Holy Mary, mother of God, pray for us sinners, now and at the hour of our death. Amen.

GLORY BE

Glory be to the Father, and to the
Son, and to the Holy Spirit, as it was
in the beginning, is now, and ever shall
be, world without end. Amen.

SECOND LUMINOUS MYSTERY
JESUS' FIRST MIRACLE

When the wine ran short, the mother of Jesus said to him, "They have no wine." [And] Jesus said to her, "Woman, how does your concern affect me? My hour has not yet come." His mother said to the servers, "Do whatever he tells you." Now there were six stone water jars there for Jewish ceremonial washings, each holding twenty to thirty gallons. Jesus told them, "Fill the jars with water." So they filled them to the brim. Then he told them, "Draw some out now and take it to the headwaiter." So they took it. And when the headwaiter tasted the water that had become wine, without knowing where it came from (although the servers who had drawn the water knew), the headwaiter called the bridegroom and said to him, "Everyone serves good wine first, and then when people have drunk freely, an inferior one; but you have kept the good wine until now" (John 2:3-10).

REFLECTION ON JESUS' FIRST MIRACLE

Mary is not addressed by name in John's Gospel. She is referred to as "the mother of Jesus," and she acts very much like a mother in this event. Although Jesus was an adult when they attended the wedding in Cana she nudged Jesus into ministry sooner than he anticipated. Mary recognized someone in need, was aware of her Son's capabilities, believed in him, and encouraged him to act. On his mother's request Jesus performed his first public miracle.

In this Scriptural passage Mary teaches us about compassion and faith. There was no more wine to serve the thirsty guests. Mary knew that with one word to Jesus, he could replenish the supply. The need would be filled and the family would avoid great embarrassment.

Jesus responded to his mother's appeal reluctantly, but he did respond and in the finest way. He changed six stone jars of water into an abundance of excellent wine. This miracle hints at a greater miracle that would come at Jesus' Last Supper with his disciples when the "wine" he shared was truly his blood.

How do you respond to the needs of people around you? When you are in need do you put your trust in Jesus? Do you allow Jesus to have control, or do you interfere in God's work?

JESUS' FIRST MIRACLE PRAYER
Jesus, I trust in you to answer all of my needs.

JESUS' FIRST MIRACLE ILLUSTRATION
Jesus changes the water into wine.

OUR FATHER

Our Father, Who art in Heaven,
Hallowed be Thy name; Thy kingdom
come; Thy will be done on earth as it
is in heaven. Give us this day our daily
bread; and forgive us our trespasses as
we forgive those who trespass against
us; and lead us not into temptation,
but deliver us from evil. Amen.

Second Decade: Pray one Hail Mary on each bead of the second decade for a total of ten Hail Marys.

HAIL MARY

Hail Mary, full of grace, the Lord is with you; blessed are you among women and blessed is the fruit of your womb, Jesus. Holy Mary, mother of God, pray for us sinners, now and at the hour of our death. Amen.

GLORY BE

Glory be to the Father, and to the
Son, and to the Holy Spirit, as it was
in the beginning, is now, and ever shall
be, world without end. Amen.

THIRD LUMINOUS MYSTERY
THE PROCLAMATION OF
THE KINGDOM OF GOD

After John had been arrested, Jesus came to Galilee proclaiming the gospel of God: "This is the time of fulfillment. The kingdom of God is at hand. Repent, and believe in the gospel" (Mark 1:14-15).

At that time the disciples approached Jesus and said, "Who is the greatest in the kingdom of heaven?" He called a child over, placed it in their midst, and said, "Amen I say to you, unless you turn and become like children, you will not enter the kingdom of heaven. Whoever humbles himself like this child is the greatest in the kingdom of heaven. And whoever receives one child such as this in my name receives me" (Matt 18:1-5).

Also see: Matt 4:17, 10:5-13; Mark 10:23-31, 12:28-34.

REFLECTION ON THE PROCLAMATION OF THE KINGDOM OF GOD

Although the third mystery highlights the Proclamation of the Kingdom of God, this concept really encompasses the entire set of Luminous Mysteries. Jesus proclaimed the Good News throughout his ministry. He said that the Kingdom of God was near. Preparation should be made immediately.

On some level the Kingdom of God is here at this very moment. It can be found where God's will is being done. It also will be found in eternal life with God. Only God knows when the final moment will come and we enter the Kingdom.

Jesus showed us the way to the Kingdom. He urged humility and conversion, the movement toward God and the avoidance of anything that draws away from that pathway. Jesus said that sins must be acknowledged, forgiveness requested, and forgiveness given. He said that the greatest commandments are to love the Lord, your God, with all your heart, with all your soul, and with all your mind (See Matt 22:37) and to love your neighbor as yourself (See Matt 22:39).

How do you love and care for the people around you? How are you preparing for the Kingdom of God?

KINGDOM OF GOD PRAYER
Jesus, you lead the way to everlasting happiness. Help me not to stray from the pathway to you.

KINGDOM OF GOD ILLUSTRATION
Jesus leads the way to the Kingdom of God.

OUR FATHER

Our Father, Who art in Heaven,
Hallowed be Thy name; Thy kingdom
come; Thy will be done on earth as it
is in heaven. Give us this day our daily
bread; and forgive us our trespasses as
we forgive those who trespass against
us; and lead us not into temptation,
but deliver us from evil. Amen.

Third Decade: Pray one Hail Mary on each bead of the third decade for a total of ten Hail Marys.

HAIL MARY

Hail Mary, full of grace, the Lord is with you; blessed are you among women and blessed is the fruit of your womb, Jesus. Holy Mary, mother of God, pray for us sinners, now and at the hour of our death. Amen.

GLORY BE

Glory be to the Father, and to the
Son, and to the Holy Spirit, as it was
in the beginning, is now, and ever shall
be, world without end. Amen.

FOURTH LUMINOUS MYSTERY
THE TRANSFIGURATION

After six days Jesus took Peter, James, and John and led them up a high mountain apart by themselves. And he was transfigured before them, and his clothes became dazzling white, such as no fuller on earth could bleach them. Then Elijah appeared to them along with Moses, and they were conversing with Jesus. Then Peter said to Jesus in reply, "Rabbi, it is good that we are here! Let us make three tents: one for you, one for Moses, and one for Elijah." He hardly knew what to say, they were so terrified. Then a cloud came, casting a shadow over them; then from the cloud came a voice, "This is my beloved Son. Listen to him." Suddenly, looking around, they no longer saw anyone but Jesus alone with them (Mark 9:2-8).

Also see: Matt 17:1-13; Luke 9:28-36.

REFLECTION ON THE TRANSFIGURATION

The Transfiguration is a revelation of God in Jesus. Jesus changed from his human form to one radiated in heavenly glory. He glowed in divine light.

God descended upon Jesus and acknowledged Jesus as God's Son. God's voice from the heavens said to listen to Jesus. Mary also said this at the wedding in Cana when she told the servants "Do whatever he tells you."

Before the Transfiguration Jesus told his disciples how he would suffer, die, and then rise on the third day, but they would not listen. They did not want to consider their Master experiencing such a tragedy, and possibly what would happen to them as Jesus' followers. The Transfiguration was a way to show Peter, James, and John that no matter how terrible things would appear, Jesus ultimately would reign as king of heaven and earth. They should listen to Jesus and look ahead with faith and hope.

Moses and Elijah, prophets and leaders of the past, appeared beside Jesus, the greatest leader of all. This was the bridge between the old and the new covenant and represented the culmination of the Law and the prophets. This was a sign of the glory that was to come.

Where and in whom do you see the light of God shining through? How do you allow God's light to be revealed? How do you listen to and follow Jesus?

TRANSFIGURATION PRAYER
Jesus, I see your glory in everyone I meet.

TRANSFIGURATION ILLUSTRATION
Jesus is the divine light of the world.

OUR FATHER

Our Father, Who art in Heaven, Hallowed be Thy name; Thy kingdom come; Thy will be done on earth as it is in heaven. Give us this day our daily bread; and forgive us our trespasses as we forgive those who trespass against us; and lead us not into temptation, but deliver us from evil. Amen.

Fourth Decade: Pray one Hail Mary on each bead of the fourth decade for a total of ten Hail Marys.

HAIL MARY

Hail Mary, full of grace, the Lord is with you; blessed are you among women and blessed is the fruit of your womb, Jesus. Holy Mary, mother of God, pray for us sinners, now and at the hour of our death. Amen.

GLORY BE

Glory be to the Father, and to the Son, and to the Holy Spirit, as it was in the beginning, is now, and ever shall be, world without end. Amen.

FIFTH LUMINOUS MYSTERY
THE INSTITUTION OF
THE EUCHARIST

While they were eating, Jesus took
bread, said the blessing, broke it, and
giving it to his disciples said, "Take
and eat; this is my body." Then he
took a cup, gave thanks, and gave it to
them, saying, "Drink from it, all of
you, for this is my blood of the
covenant, which will be shed on
behalf of many for the forgiveness of
sins. I tell you, from now on I shall
not drink this fruit of the vine until
the day when I drink it with you new
in the kingdom of my Father." Then,
after singing a hymn, they went out to
the Mount of Olives (Matt 26:26-30).

Also see: Mark 14:22-26; Luke 22:14-20.

REFLECTION ON THE INSTITUTION
OF THE EUCHARIST

The last meal Jesus shared with his disciples before his death was the annual remembrance of the Passover in Egypt. The Passover happened when the Israelites had been held captive by the Egyptians. God sent ten plagues before the Egyptians would release the people. With the last plague the Lord slew every first born Egyptian human and animal. The Israelites were spared because they obeyed the Lord and applied blood from an unblemished lamb on their doorposts and ate the roasted meat (See Exod 12).

At the Last Supper Jesus said that the bread and wine he shared was his body and blood. He was the unblemished lamb whose blood would be shed for the salvation of the people. He was, and is, the Lamb of God who takes away the sin of the world.

Jesus told the disciples that the next time they would eat together would be in the kingdom of his Father. This signaled the new exodus into the Promised Land, which is the Kingdom of God.

The Eucharist is the gift of salvation, our freedom from sin. How often do you share in the Eucharist? How often do you thank God for the gift of Jesus? How often do you thank Christ for our salvation?

EUCHARISTIC PRAYER
Lord Jesus, you feed my body, mind, and soul.

EUCHARISTIC ILLUSTRATION
The bread and wine of the Eucharist becomes the Body and Blood of Jesus Christ.

OUR FATHER

Our Father, Who art in Heaven, Hallowed be Thy name; Thy kingdom come; Thy will be done on earth as it is in heaven. Give us this day our daily bread; and forgive us our trespasses as we forgive those who trespass against us; and lead us not into temptation, but deliver us from evil. Amen.

Fifth Decade: Pray one Hail Mary on each bead of the fifth decade for a total of ten Hail Marys.

HAIL MARY

Hail Mary, full of grace, the Lord is with you; blessed are you among women and blessed is the fruit of your womb, Jesus. Holy Mary, mother of God, pray for us sinners, now and at the hour of our death. Amen.

GLORY BE

Glory be to the Father, and to the
Son, and to the Holy Spirit, as it was
in the beginning, is now, and ever shall
be, world without end. Amen.

HAIL, HOLY QUEEN

Hail, holy Queen, Mother of mercy;
our life, our sweetness and our hope.
To you do we cry, poor banished
children of Eve. To you do we send
up our sighs, mourning and weeping
in this valley of tears. Turn then, most
gracious Advocate, your eyes of
mercy toward us, and after this our
exile, show unto us the blessed fruit
of your womb, Jesus. O clement, O
loving, O sweet Virgin Mary.

V: Pray for us, O holy Mother of
God.

R: That we may become worthy of
the promises of Christ. Amen.

SIGN OF THE CROSS

In the name of the Father,
and of the Son,
and of the Holy Spirit.
Amen.

THE ROSARY

WITH THE

SORROWFUL

MYSTERIES

SIGN OF THE CROSS

In the name of the Father,
and of the Son,
and of the Holy Spirit.
Amen.

THE APOSTLES' CREED

I believe in God, the Father Almighty,
Creator of heaven and earth; and in
Jesus Christ, His only son, Our Lord,
who was conceived by the Holy Spirit,
born of the Virgin Mary, suffered
under Pontius Pilate, was crucified,
died, and was buried. He descended
into hell; the third day He arose again
from the dead; He ascended into
heaven and sits at the right hand of
God, the Father Almighty; from
thence He shall come to judge the
living and the dead. I believe in the
Holy Spirit, the Holy Catholic church,
the communion of saints, the forgiveness of sins, the resurrection of the
body and life everlasting. Amen.

OUR FATHER

Our Father, Who art in Heaven,
Hallowed be Thy name; Thy kingdom
come; Thy will be done on earth as it
is in heaven. Give us this day our daily
bread; and forgive us our trespasses as
we forgive those who trespass against
us; and lead us not into temptation,
but deliver us from evil. Amen

HAIL MARY

Hail Mary, full of grace, the Lord is with you; blessed are you among women and blessed is the fruit of your womb, Jesus. Holy Mary, mother of God, pray for us sinners, now and at the hour of our death. Amen.

HAIL MARY

Hail Mary, full of grace, the Lord is with you; blessed are you among women and blessed is the fruit of your womb, Jesus. Holy Mary, mother of God, pray for us sinners, now and at the hour of our death. Amen.

HAIL MARY

Hail Mary, full of grace, the Lord is with you; blessed are you among women and blessed is the fruit of your womb, Jesus. Holy Mary, mother of God, pray for us sinners, now and at the hour of our death. Amen.

GLORY BE

Glory be to the Father, and to the
Son, and to the Holy Spirit, as it was
in the beginning, is now, and ever shall
be, world without end. Amen.

FIRST SORROWFUL MYSTERY
THE AGONY IN THE GARDEN

Then going out he went, as was his
custom, to the Mount of Olives, and
the disciples followed him. When he
arrived at the place he said to them,
"Pray that you may not undergo the
test." After withdrawing about a
stone's throw from them and kneeling,
he prayed, saying, "Father, if you are
willing, take this cup away from me;
still, not my will but yours be done."
[And to strengthen him an angel from
heaven appeared to him. He was in
such agony and he prayed so fervently
that his sweat became like drops of
blood falling on the ground.] When he
rose from prayer and returned to his
disciples, he found them sleeping
from grief. He said to them, "Why are
you sleeping? Get up and pray that
you may not undergo the test" (Luke
22:39-46).

*Also see: Matthew 26:36-46;
Mark 14:32-42.*

REFLECTION ON
THE AGONY IN THE GARDEN

Just prior to his arrest, Jesus went with his disciples into a garden to pray. Jesus was in misery knowing what was about to happen. He asked God to spare him. But he also said that he would accept whatever his Father wanted of him.

The intense sadness, stress, and perhaps fear that Jesus experienced is evident. Luke describes Jesus' agony as so severe that his sweat became like drops of blood. Both Matthew and Mark's Gospels say that Jesus told his disciples how he felt and begged for their support.

However, the disciples did not comprehend the magnitude of what was to occur. Instead of praying with him, they fell asleep. Jesus' closest companions failed him in his greatest time of need.

God does not fail us. Jesus teaches us to go to the Father when we are sad, worried, or troubled. Prayer is powerful. God will hear and answer us, although sometimes in ways other than what we had hoped.

Many innocent people suffer incomprehensible illnesses, tragedies, and heartaches. How have you suffered? Who do you know that is in pain? How do you pray to the Father when you are troubled or when others are? Do you do what God asks of you, no matter what that may mean?

AGONY IN THE GARDEN PRAYER
Father, help me. I need you and trust in you.

AGONY IN THE GARDEN ILLUSTRATION
Tormented with grief, Jesus prays to his Father.

OUR FATHER

Our Father, Who art in Heaven,
Hallowed be Thy name; Thy kingdom
come; Thy will be done on earth as it
is in heaven. Give us this day our daily
bread; and forgive us our trespasses as
we forgive those who trespass against
us; and lead us not into temptation,
but deliver us from evil. Amen.

First Decade: Pray one Hail Mary on each bead of the first decade for a total of ten Hail Marys.

HAIL MARY

Hail Mary, full of grace, the Lord is with you; blessed are you among women and blessed is the fruit of your womb, Jesus. Holy Mary, mother of God, pray for us sinners, now and at the hour of our death. Amen.

GLORY BE

Glory be to the Father, and to the Son, and to the Holy Spirit, as it was in the beginning, is now, and ever shall be, world without end. Amen.

SECOND
SORROWFUL MYSTERY
THE SCOURGING AT
THE PILLAR

Now on the occasion of the feast he used to release to them one prisoner whom they requested. A man called Barabbas was then in prison along with the rebels who had committed murder in a rebellion. The crowd came forward and began to ask him to do for them as he was accustomed. Pilate answered, "Do you want me to release to you the king of the Jews?" For he knew that it was out of envy that the chief priests had handed him over. But the chief priests stirred up the crowd to have him release Barabbas for them instead. Pilate again said to them in reply, "Then what [do you want] me to do with [the man you call] the king of the Jews?" They shouted again, "Crucify him." Pilate said to them, "Why? What evil has he done?" They only shouted the louder, "Crucify him." So Pilate, wishing to satisfy the crowd, released Barabbas to them and, after he had Jesus scourged, handed him over to be crucified (Mark 15:6-15).

REFLECTION ON
THE SCOURGING AT THE PILLAR

Each year during Passover it was the custom to release one prisoner. Pilate encouraged the crowd to choose the innocent Jesus, but the chief priests rallied for Barabbas, and Pilate hadn't the courage to oppose the angry crowd. Jesus was sent away to be scourged and crucified.

The gospels don't give the gruesome details of the scourging, but historically the Romans beat prisoners with a flagellum, a whip made of leather with pieces of bone, lead, or bronze tied at the ends. Victims would go into shock from the pain or bleed to death.

The markings on the Shroud of Turin, the cloth thought to have been wrapped around Jesus' dead body, suggests that he may have been whipped more than 100 times. Jewish law only allowed 40 lashes; however, the Romans had no limit for slaves and noncitizens.

When I receive the Blood of Christ of the Eucharist, I tremble at the thought of the blood Jesus shed at the scourging. Each drop of precious blood is a gift Jesus willingly offered for you and me.

How do you show your appreciation for Jesus' sacrifice? Do you intervene on the behalf of the innocent, or are you like Pilate and look away?

SCOURGING AT THE PILLAR PRAYER
Lord, give me the strength and courage to defend and protect the persecuted people of the world.

SCOURGING AT THE PILLAR ILLUSTRATION
Jesus is tied to the post and brutally beaten.

OUR FATHER

Our Father, Who art in Heaven,
Hallowed be Thy name; Thy kingdom
come; Thy will be done on earth as it
is in heaven. Give us this day our daily
bread; and forgive us our trespasses as
we forgive those who trespass against
us; and lead us not into temptation,
but deliver us from evil. Amen.

Second Decade: Pray one Hail Mary on each bead of the second decade for a total of ten Hail Marys.

HAIL MARY

Hail Mary, full of grace, the Lord is with you; blessed are you among women and blessed is the fruit of your womb, Jesus. Holy Mary, mother of God, pray for us sinners, now and at the hour of our death. Amen.

GLORY BE

Glory be to the Father, and to the
Son, and to the Holy Spirit, as it was
in the beginning, is now, and ever shall
be, world without end. Amen.

THIRD
SORROWFUL MYSTERY
THE CROWNING
WITH THORNS

The soldiers led him away inside the palace, that is, the praetorium, and assembled the whole cohort. They clothed him in purple and, weaving a crown of thorns, placed it on him. They began to salute him with, "Hail, King of the Jews!" and kept striking his head with a reed and spitting upon him. They knelt before him in homage. And when they had mocked him, they stripped him of the purple cloak, dressed him in his own clothes, and led him out to crucify him (Mark 15:16-20).

Also see: Matt 27:29; John 19:2-16.

REFLECTION ON
THE CROWNING WITH THORNS

This mystery is a reflection on the use and abuse of leadership and power. Jesus truly is king of all kings; however, he never dressed or acted royally. He was a servant leader–humble, gentle, merciful, and forgiving.

After being severely beaten, Jesus' physical and emotional abuse was continued by an entire military battalion. He was spat on and beaten with a rod. He was stripped in front of the men and "adorned" in a regal robe and a crown of thorns in mockery of his role as the messiah, the anointed king of the Jews.

Jesus' crown is thought to have been a mass of long, spiky thorns. The head has many blood vessels and nerves. It must have been very painful for Jesus to have had this pressed onto his scalp.

Jesus also endured emotional pain, which can be more hurtful than physical abuse. That is where we are robbed of our self-esteem, joy in living, individuality, and faith and trust in humanity. Such abuse leaves us crippled and unable to pull ourselves out of the depths of despair.

Jesus suffered at least as severely as any other human being has ever experienced. How have you suffered? How have you caused suffering?

CROWNING WITH THORNS PRAYER
When I feel as though I am at the mercy of everyone, Father I know you are with me.

CROWNING WITH THORNS ILLUSTRATION
Jesus bears the pain of physical and emotional torture.

OUR FATHER

Our Father, Who art in Heaven, Hallowed be Thy name; Thy kingdom come; Thy will be done on earth as it is in heaven. Give us this day our daily bread; and forgive us our trespasses as we forgive those who trespass against us; and lead us not into temptation, but deliver us from evil. Amen.

Third Decade: Pray one Hail Mary on each bead of the third decade for a total of ten Hail Marys.

HAIL MARY

Hail Mary, full of grace, the Lord is with you; blessed are you among women and blessed is the fruit of your womb, Jesus. Holy Mary, mother of God, pray for us sinners, now and at the hour of our death. Amen.

GLORY BE

Glory be to the Father, and to the
Son, and to the Holy Spirit, as it was
in the beginning, is now, and ever shall
be, world without end. Amen.

FOURTH
SORROWFUL MYSTERY
THE CARRYING
OF THE CROSS

As they led him away they took
hold of a certain Simon, a Cyrenian,
who was coming in from the country;
and after laying the cross on him, they
made him carry it behind Jesus. A
large crowd of people followed Jesus,
including many women who mourned
and lamented him. Jesus turned to
them and said, "Daughters of Jerusalem, do not weep for me; weep
instead for yourselves and for your
children, for indeed, the days are
coming when people will say, 'Blessed
are the barren, the wombs that never
bore and the breasts that never
nursed.' At that time people will say to
the mountains, 'Fall upon us!' and to
the hills, 'Cover us!' for if these things
are done when the wood is green what
will happen when it is dry?" (Luke
23:26-31).

Also see: Matt 27:32; Mark 15:21;
John 19:17.

REFLECTION ON
THE CARRYING OF THE CROSS

Jesus must have been too weak to carry his cross for the Romans to demand that Simon help him. Yet even in his frail condition Jesus showed concern for humanity. He instructed the mourners not to cry for him but rather focus on repentance and the salvation of their children.

The carrying of the crossbar by prisoners on the path to execution was humiliating for bystanders to witness. Supporters of Jesus were powerless to rescue him. They may have been fearful of retaliation by the guards if they showed any objection to the proceedings.

An Austrian woman once told me of an experience she had as a child during World War II. Every day she was required to pass a concentration camp to and from school. She said she has never overcome the sense of terror and helplessness in her inability to prevent the atrocities she saw inflicted upon the captives.

Evil may be at its most horrendous point when it forces people to witness or participate in brutality. Are you an abuser, witness, victim, or rescuer? Do you participate in public ridicule or gossip? Do you bully or intimidate the weak?

CARRYING OF THE CROSS PRAYER
May there always be angels to help me carry my crosses, and may I have the courage to help other people carry theirs.

CARRYING OF THE CROSS ILLUSTRATION
Jesus drags his heavy cross to his own crucifixion.

OUR FATHER

Our Father, Who art in Heaven,
Hallowed be Thy name; Thy kingdom
come; Thy will be done on earth as it
is in heaven. Give us this day our daily
bread; and forgive us our trespasses as
we forgive those who trespass against
us; and lead us not into temptation,
but deliver us from evil. Amen.

Fourth Decade: Pray one Hail Mary on each bead of the fourth decade for a total of ten Hail Marys.

HAIL MARY

Hail Mary, full of grace, the Lord is with you; blessed are you among women and blessed is the fruit of your womb, Jesus. Holy Mary, mother of God, pray for us sinners, now and at the hour of our death. Amen.

GLORY BE

Glory be to the Father, and to the
Son, and to the Holy Spirit, as it was
in the beginning, is now, and ever shall
be, world without end. Amen.

FIFTH SORROWFUL MYSTERY
THE CRUCIFIXION

And about three o'clock Jesus cried out in a loud voice, "*Eli, Eli, lema sabachthani?*" which means, "My God, my God, why have you forsaken me?" Some of the bystanders who heard it said, "This one is calling for Elijah." Immediately one of them ran to get a sponge; he soaked it in wine, and putting it on a reed, gave it to him to drink. But the rest said, "Wait, let us see if Elijah comes to save him." But Jesus cried out again in a loud voice, and gave up his spirit. And behold, the veil of the sanctuary was torn in two from top to bottom. The earth quaked, rocks were split, tombs were opened, and the bodies of many saints who had fallen asleep were raised. And coming forth from their tombs after his resurrection, they entered the holy city and appeared to many. The centurion and the men with him who were keeping watch over Jesus feared greatly when they saw the earthquake and all that was happening, and they said, "Truly, this was the Son of God!" (Matt 27:46-54).
Also see: Mark 15:22-41; Luke 23:33-43; John 19: 17-30.

151

REFLECTION ON THE CRUCIFIXION

Crucifixion was a common form of execution in the early centuries. It was demoralizing and humiliating for witnesses, executioners, and especially victims. Jesus, like thousands of others, was beaten, taunted, and hung naked until he suffocated. Jesus' legs were not broken, as often done to prisoners on the cross, but after his death a soldier lanced his side.

Reading the complete crucifixion and death passages from all four gospels is very insightful because each one has a slightly different focus. Matthew and Mark's Gospels say that Jesus asked God why he was abandoned. Luke's Gospel tells us the "good" thief recognized Jesus as savior and that Jesus asked God to forgive his enemies. In the Gospel of John it is written that Jesus told his mother and the disciple John to care for one another.

We can never say that God does not understand how we feel. Jesus, God's Son, in His human nature, lived and died as painfully as any human being has. He suffered public humiliation, the emotional loss of the support from friends, the embarrassment of being tortured in his mother's presence, and horrendous physical abuse.

How have you been persecuted? What pain have you caused others? How do you care for the lonely, helpless, and persecuted?

THE CRUCIFIXION PRAYER
Thank you, Jesus, for suffering and dying for me.

THE CRUCIFIXION ILLUSTRATION
Jesus bore the salvation of the world on his shoulders.

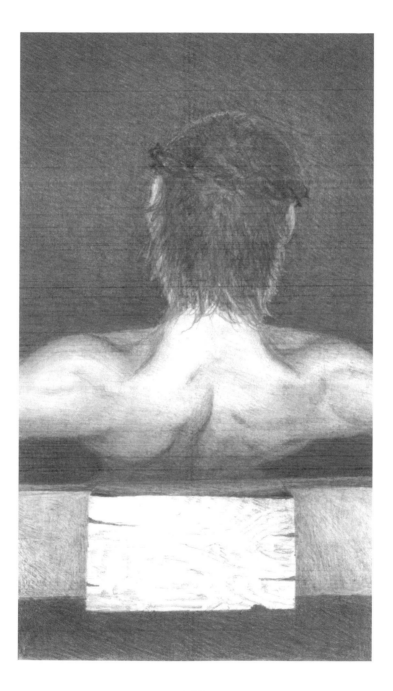

153

OUR FATHER

Our Father, Who art in Heaven,
Hallowed be Thy name; Thy kingdom
come; Thy will be done on earth as it
is in heaven. Give us this day our daily
bread; and forgive us our trespasses as
we forgive those who trespass against
us; and lead us not into temptation,
but deliver us from evil. Amen.

Fifth Decade: Pray one Hail Mary on each bead of the fifth decade for a total of ten Hail Marys.

HAIL MARY

Hail Mary, full of grace, the Lord is with you; blessed are you among women and blessed is the fruit of your womb, Jesus. Holy Mary, mother of God, pray for us sinners, now and at the hour of our death. Amen.

GLORY BE

Glory be to the Father, and to the
Son, and to the Holy Spirit, as it was
in the beginning, is now, and ever shall
be, world without end. Amen.

HAIL, HOLY QUEEN

Hail, holy Queen, Mother of mercy;
our life, our sweetness and our hope.
To you do we cry, poor banished
children of Eve. To you do we send
up our sighs, mourning and weeping
in this valley of tears. Turn then, most
gracious Advocate, your eyes of
mercy toward us, and after this our
exile, show unto us the blessed fruit
of your womb, Jesus. O clement, O
loving, O sweet Virgin Mary.

V: Pray for us, O holy Mother of
God.

R: That we may become worthy of
the promises of Christ. Amen.

SIGN OF THE CROSS

In the name of the Father,
and of the Son,
and of the Holy Spirit.
Amen.

THE ROSARY

WITH THE

GLORIOUS

MYSTERIES

SIGN OF THE CROSS

In the name of the Father,
and of the Son,
and of the Holy Spirit.
Amen.

THE APOSTLES' CREED

I believe in God, the Father Almighty,
Creator of heaven and earth; and in
Jesus Christ, His only son, Our Lord,
who was conceived by the Holy Spirit,
born of the Virgin Mary, suffered
under Pontius Pilate, was crucified,
died, and was buried. He descended
into hell; the third day He arose again
from the dead; He ascended into
heaven and sits at the right hand of
God, the Father Almighty; from
thence He shall come to judge the
living and the dead. I believe in the
Holy Spirit, the Holy Catholic church,
the communion of saints, the forgiveness of sins, the resurrection of the
body and life everlasting. Amen.

OUR FATHER

Our Father, Who art in Heaven, Hallowed be Thy name; Thy kingdom come; Thy will be done on earth as it is in heaven. Give us this day our daily bread; and forgive us our trespasses as we forgive those who trespass against us; and lead us not into temptation, but deliver us from evil. Amen

HAIL MARY

Hail Mary, full of grace, the Lord is
with you; blessed are you among
women and blessed is the fruit of
your womb, Jesus. Holy Mary, mother
of God, pray for us sinners, now and
at the hour of our death. Amen.

HAIL MARY

Hail Mary, full of grace, the Lord is
with you; blessed are you among
women and blessed is the fruit of
your womb, Jesus. Holy Mary, mother
of God, pray for us sinners, now and
at the hour of our death. Amen.

HAIL MARY

Hail Mary, full of grace, the Lord is
with you; blessed are you among
women and blessed is the fruit of
your womb, Jesus. Holy Mary, mother
of God, pray for us sinners, now and
at the hour of our death. Amen.

GLORY BE

Glory be to the Father, and to the
Son, and to the Holy Spirit, as it was
in the beginning, is now, and ever shall
be, world without end. Amen.

FIRST GLORIOUS MYSTERY
THE RESURRECTION

Thomas, called Didymus, one of the Twelve, was not with them when Jesus came. So the other disciples said to him, "We have seen the Lord." But he said to them, "Unless I see the mark of the nails in his hands and put my finger into the nailmarks and put my hand into his side, I will not believe." Now a week later his disciples were again inside and Thomas was with them. Jesus came, although the doors were locked, and stood in their midst and said, "Peace be with you." Then he said to Thomas, "Put your finger here and see my hands, and bring your hand and put it into my side, and do not be unbelieving, but believe." Thomas answered and said to him, "My Lord and my God!" Jesus said to him, "Have you come to believe because you have seen me? Blessed are those who have not seen and have believed" (John 20:24-29).

Also see: Matt 28:1-10; Mark 16:1-18; Luke 24:1-49.

REFLECTION ON THE RESURRECTION

John's Gospel says that Mary Magdalene went to the tomb to anoint Jesus' dead body but found the tomb empty. She thought that the body had been stolen and began to cry when she turned around and saw Jesus.

Mary Magdalene told the disciples that Jesus had risen; but they did not understand. Thomas said that he needed proof that Jesus truly had risen from the dead. Our "proof" is in the women's testimony of the empty tomb and lack of any human remains of Jesus' dead body. Mary was able to hold Jesus, Thomas touched his wounds, and Luke's Gospel says that Jesus ate a piece of fish (24:42-43).

Numerous first century people became disciples of Christ following the Resurrection. They did so at great risk of their own persecution, because they had no doubt that Jesus, the Christ, which means the Anointed One, came back to life after being tortured and crucified, dying, and enclosed in a tomb for three days.

Jesus said, "I am the resurrection and the life; whoever believes in me, even if he dies, will live, and everyone who lives and believes in me will never die" (John 11:25-26). The Resurrection is one of our greatest mysteries and signs of hope. How do you prove your belief in and love for Jesus? How do you testify to the Resurrection?

RESURRECTION PRAYER
I am alive in the truth of Jesus' Resurrection.

RESURRECTION ILLUSTRATION
Jesus' hands reveal the marks of the crucifixion.

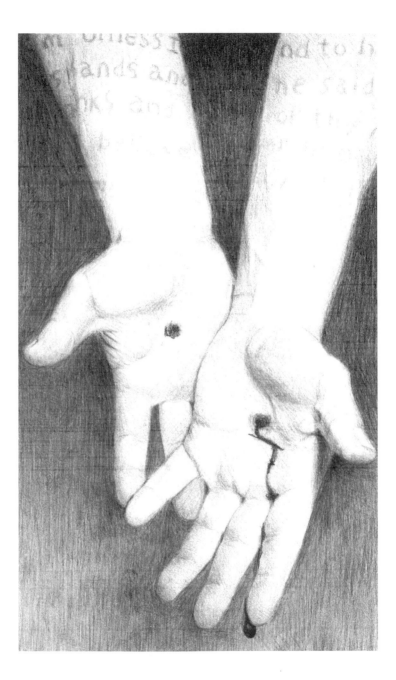

OUR FATHER

Our Father, Who art in Heaven,
Hallowed be Thy name; Thy kingdom
come; Thy will be done on earth as it
is in heaven. Give us this day our daily
bread; and forgive us our trespasses as
we forgive those who trespass against
us; and lead us not into temptation,
but deliver us from evil. Amen.

First Decade: Pray one Hail Mary on each bead of the first decade for a total of ten Hail Marys.

HAIL MARY

Hail Mary, full of grace, the Lord is with you; blessed are you among women and blessed is the fruit of your womb, Jesus. Holy Mary, mother of God, pray for us sinners, now and at the hour of our death. Amen.

GLORY BE

Glory be to the Father, and to the
Son, and to the Holy Spirit, as it was
in the beginning, is now, and ever shall
be, world without end. Amen.

SECOND
GLORIOUS MYSTERY
THE ASCENSION

When they had gathered together
they asked him, "Lord, are you at this
time going to restore the kingdom to
Israel?" He answered them, "It is not
for you to know the times or seasons
that the Father has established by his
own authority. But you will receive
power when the holy Spirit comes
upon you, and you will be my witnesses in Jerusalem, throughout Judea
and Samaria, and to the ends of the
earth." When he had said this, as they
were looking on, he was lifted up, and
a cloud took him from their sight.
While they were looking intently at the
sky as he was going, suddenly two
men dressed in white garments stood
beside them. They said, "Men of
Galilee, why are you standing there
looking at the sky? This Jesus who has
been taken up from you into heaven
will return in the same way as you
have seen him going into heaven"
(Acts 1:6-11).

Also see: Mark 16:19; Luke 24:50-51,
1 Tim 3:16.

REFLECTION ON THE ASCENSION

The restoration of the kingdom to the Israelites had been promised since the time of King David. Jesus also talked about a kingdom, the Kingdom of God. Of course the disciples expected the resurrected Messiah to reinstate this kingdom, or establish the new kingdom he described, before his ascension.

But when the disciples asked about it, Jesus replied that the time or season that this would happen was not for them to know. With that, Jesus disappeared into the clouds. Mark's Gospel says that Jesus was seated at the right hand of God (16:19).

Leaving things for God to do in God's time and ways is challenging for earthly beings. We plan our day, our weeks, and our lives. We want to know exactly when and how things are going to happen.

Yet, so much about faith cannot be confined to a human time frame and structure. We have to believe and trust. We have to "let go and let God," as the saying goes.

Jesus told the disciples to focus on witnessing to his teachings. They were to remember Jesus' ways and words and proclaim them. As disciples of Christ, we take on that role also. How do you spread the Gospels through your actions and words? What kind of disciple are you?

ASCENSION PRAYER
Holy Spirit give me the strength to be a powerful disciple of Christ.

ASCENSION ILLUSTRATION
Jesus ascends into the heavens.

OUR FATHER

Our Father, Who art in Heaven, Hallowed be Thy name; Thy kingdom come; Thy will be done on earth as it is in heaven. Give us this day our daily bread; and forgive us our trespasses as we forgive those who trespass against us; and lead us not into temptation, but deliver us from evil. Amen.

Second Decade: Pray one Hail Mary on each bead of the second decade for a total of ten Hail Marys.

HAIL MARY

Hail Mary, full of grace, the Lord is with you; blessed are you among women and blessed is the fruit of your womb, Jesus. Holy Mary, mother of God, pray for us sinners, now and at the hour of our death. Amen.

GLORY BE

Glory be to the Father, and to the
Son, and to the Holy Spirit, as it was
in the beginning, is now, and ever shall
be, world without end. Amen.

THIRD GLORIOUS MYSTERY
THE DESCENT OF
THE HOLY SPIRIT

When the time for Pentecost was
fulfilled, they were all in one place
together. And suddenly there came
from the sky a noise like a strong
driving wind, and it filled the entire
house in which they were. Then there
appeared to them tongues as of fire,
which parted and came to rest on each
one of them. And they were all filled
with the holy Spirit and began to
speak in different tongues, as the
Spirit enabled them to proclaim (Acts
2:1-4).

REFLECTION ON
THE DESCENT OF THE HOLY SPIRIT

The apostles, Mary, and some other women had gathered in the upper room in Jerusalem to celebrate the feast of Pentecost. Suddenly the Holy Spirit made a dramatic entrance. A noise like strong wind filled the house. *Ruah* is the Hebrew word for the Holy Spirit. It means breath of God. God's Spirit breathed right into the room. Fire appeared, split into little flames, and rested upon each of the people in the room. Everyone was filled with the Spirit and began to speak in different languages.

God became incarnate (became flesh) in Jesus to show creation how to live. After Jesus ascended back to heaven the Holy Spirit empowered disciples to spread the Word in multiple ways according to their gifts. The spiritual gifts include wisdom, knowledge, faith, healing, mighty deeds, prophecy, discernment of spirits, and speaking and praying in tongues (See 1Cor 12:8-10). The fruits (the results of the gifts) of the Holy Spirit are love, joy, peace, patience, kindness, generosity, faithfulness, gentleness, and self-control (See Gal 5:22-23).

What are your gifts? How do you use them?

DESCENT OF THE HOLY SPIRIT PRAYER
Holy Spirit guide me to the full and holy use of the gifts with which You have blessed me.

DESCENT OF THE HOLY SPIRIT
ILLUSTRATION
The Holy Spirit blesses the world with many gifts.

179

OUR FATHER

Our Father, Who art in Heaven,
Hallowed be Thy name; Thy kingdom
come; Thy will be done on earth as it
is in heaven. Give us this day our daily
bread; and forgive us our trespasses as
we forgive those who trespass against
us; and lead us not into temptation,
but deliver us from evil. Amen.

Third Decade: Pray one Hail Mary on each bead of the third decade for a total of ten Hail Marys.

HAIL MARY

Hail Mary, full of grace, the Lord is with you; blessed are you among women and blessed is the fruit of your womb, Jesus. Holy Mary, mother of God, pray for us sinners, now and at the hour of our death. Amen.

GLORY BE

Glory be to the Father, and to the
Son, and to the Holy Spirit, as it was
in the beginning, is now, and ever shall
be, world without end. Amen.

FOURTH
GLORIOUS MYSTERY
THE ASSUMPTION

The Second Vatican Council wrote in the "Dogmatic Constitution on the Church," *Lumen Gentium*, "the Immaculate Virgin, preserved free from all stain of original sin, was taken up body and soul into heavenly glory, when her earthly life was over, and exalted by the Lord as Queen over all things" (59).

See: *Vatican Council II, Volume 1. Revised Edition: The Conciliar and Post Conciliar Documents.*

REFLECTION ON THE ASSUMPTION

The Assumption of Mary is not explicitly found in Scripture, but it is drawn from it. The belief was established by the early second century. Liturgical feasts honoring Mary's Assumption were being celebrated in Syria by the sixth century and common among all Christian communities by the eighth. It wasn't until 1950 that Pope Pius XII defined the dogma of the Assumption of Mary in the papal bull *Munificentissimus Deus*.

Some Scripture references to support the belief in the Assumption of Mary are Psalm 132, Isaiah 60:13, and Revelation 12:6.

The resurrection of the body is promised to all good people at the end of times. Church doctrine says that God took Mary's body and soul up into heaven immediately at the end of her life because of her holiness and position as mother of Jesus. According to Scripture the prophets Enoch (Heb 11:5) and Elijah (2 Kings 2:11) also were assumed into heaven.

We also hope to be taken to heaven at the end of our lives. How are you preparing for this journey? Are you ready to be judged by your faith and works? Do you think Christ will welcome you into eternal life?

ASSUMPTION PRAYER
Holy Mary, Mother of God, pray for me now and at the hour of my death.

ASSUMPTION ILLUSTRATION
As rain falls from the heavens Mary's Assumption reflects on the waters of the earth.

185

OUR FATHER

Our Father, Who art in Heaven,
Hallowed be Thy name; Thy kingdom
come; Thy will be done on earth as it
is in heaven. Give us this day our daily
bread; and forgive us our trespasses as
we forgive those who trespass against
us; and lead us not into temptation,
but deliver us from evil. Amen.

Fourth Decade: Pray one Hail Mary on each bead of the fourth decade for a total of ten Hail Marys.

HAIL MARY

Hail Mary, full of grace, the Lord is with you; blessed are you among women and blessed is the fruit of your womb, Jesus. Holy Mary, mother of God, pray for us sinners, now and at the hour of our death. Amen.

GLORY BE

Glory be to the Father, and to the
Son, and to the Holy Spirit, as it was
in the beginning, is now, and ever shall
be, world without end. Amen.

FIFTH GLORIOUS MYSTERY
THE CORONATION

A great sign appeared in the sky, a woman clothed with the sun, with the moon under her feet, and on her head a crown of twelve stars. She was with child and wailed aloud in pain as she labored to give birth. Then another sign appeared in the sky; it was a huge red dragon, with seven heads and ten horns, and on its heads were seven diadems. Its tail swept away a third of the stars in the sky and hurled them down to the earth. Then the dragon stood before the woman about to give birth, to devour her child when she gave birth (Rev 12:1-4).

REFLECTION ON THE CORONATION

The Book of Revelation is symbolically written. The Traditional Catholic interpretation is that the woman in the story is Mary. She is crowned "Queen" and "Our Lady." The twelve stars represent the twelve tribes of Israel and the twelve apostles. The dragon is an opposing force of God and an ancient symbol of chaos.

Mary's title "Queen of Heaven and Earth" is not found in Scripture or a defined Church dogma. However, Mary lovingly has been referred to as queen by the faithful since at least the fifth century. In ancient times a king's mother, not his wife, reigned as queen. (See 1 Kings 2.) Royal status is awarded to Mary because of the honor due to her as the Mother of Jesus the King.

Some of Mary's many royal titles include; Queen of Saints, Queen of Peace, Queen of Angels, and Queen of Mercy. We are members of the Kingdom of God. Mary is our ever-loving, Queen Mother who prays for all her children. Her wish is for us to devoutly follow her Son, Jesus, and love and care for each other.

How do you honor Our Lady and Queen? How do you follow her example of love for all of God's creations?

CORONATION PRAYER
Mary Queen of Heaven and Earth, have mercy on us.
Mary Queen of Peace and Love, pray for us.

CORONATION ILLUSTRATION
Mary is queen of heaven and earth.

OUR FATHER

Our Father, Who art in Heaven,
Hallowed be Thy name; Thy kingdom
come; Thy will be done on earth as it
is in heaven. Give us this day our daily
bread; and forgive us our trespasses as
we forgive those who trespass against
us; and lead us not into temptation,
but deliver us from evil. Amen.

Fifth Decade: Pray one Hail Mary on each bead of the fifth decade for a total of ten Hail Marys.

HAIL MARY

Hail Mary, full of grace, the Lord is with you; blessed are you among women and blessed is the fruit of your womb, Jesus. Holy Mary, mother of God, pray for us sinners, now and at the hour of our death. Amen.

GLORY BE

Glory be to the Father, and to the
Son, and to the Holy Spirit, as it was
in the beginning, is now, and ever shall
be, world without end. Amen.

HAIL, HOLY QUEEN

Hail, holy Queen, Mother of mercy; our life, our sweetness and our hope. To you do we cry, poor banished children of Eve. To you do we send up our sighs, mourning and weeping in this valley of tears. Turn then, most gracious Advocate, your eyes of mercy toward us, and after this our exile, show unto us the blessed fruit of your womb, Jesus. O clement, O loving, O sweet Virgin Mary.

V: Pray for us, O holy Mother of God.

R: That we may become worthy of the promises of Christ. Amen.

SIGN OF THE CROSS

In the name of the Father,
and of the Son,
and of the Holy Spirit.
Amen.

The Rosary with the Glorious Mysteries

The Rosary Prayer by Prayer

PART III

MORE INFORMATION

AND RESOURCES

ADDITIONAL PRAYERS PRAYED WITH THE ROSARY

In 1917 Blessed Mother appeared six times to three young shepherds: Lucia, Francisco, and Jacinta. Mary asked them to pray the rosary every day for peace and add the following prayer to each mystery. This prayer is commonly said after the Glory Be.

FATIMA PRAYER

O my Jesus, forgive us our sins. Save us from the fires of hell. Lead all souls to heaven, especially those in most need of your mercy. Amen.

The Next Prayers May Be Said After the Rosary

CLOSING PRAYER

O God, Whose only begotten son, by His life, death, and resurrection has purchased for us the rewards of eternal life; grant, we beseech thee, that meditating upon these mysteries of the most holy rosary of the Blessed Virgin Mary, we may imitate what they contain and obtain what they promise through the same Christ our Lord. Amen

PRAYER TO SAINT MICHAEL

Saint Michael the Archangel, defend us in battle. Be our safeguard against the wickedness and snares of the devil. May God rebuke him, we humbly pray; and do you, O Prince of the heavenly host, by the divine power of God, thrust into hell Satan and all the other evil spirits who wander through the world seeking the ruin of souls. Amen.

MEMORARE

Remember, O most gracious Virgin Mary, that never was it known that anyone who fled to your protection, implored your help, or sought your intercession was left unaided. Inspired with this confidence, I fly unto you, O Virgin of virgins, my Mother. To you I come; before you I stand, sinful and sorrowful. O Mother of the Word Incarnate, despise not my petitions, but in your mercy hear and answer me. Amen.

Additional Prayers Prayed with the Rosary

THE MAGNIFICAT
MARY'S SONG OF PRAISE (LUKE 1:46-55)

My soul magnifies the Lord,
    and my spirit rejoices in God /my Saviour,
for he has looked with favour on the /lowliness of his
    servant. /Surely, from now on all generations
    will call me blessed;
for the Mighty One has done great /things for me,
    and holy is his name.
His mercy is for those who fear him
    from generation to generation.
He has shown strength with /his arm;
    he has scattered the proud in the
    thoughts of their hearts.
He has brought down the powerful
    from their thrones, /and lifted up the lowly;
he has filled the hungry with /good things,
    and sent the rich away empty.
He has helped his servant Israel,
    in remembrance of his mercy,
according to the promise he made to /our ancestors,
    to Abraham and to his descendants /for ever.

LITANY OF
THE BLESSED VIRGIN MARY

Lord, have mercy	Lord, have mercy
Christ, have mercy	Christ, have mercy
Lord, have mercy	Lord, have mercy
God our Father in heaven	have mercy on us
God the Son, Redeemer of the world	have mercy on us
God the Holy Spirit	have mercy on us
Holy Trinity, one God	have mercy on us
Holy Mary	pray for us
Holy Mother of God	pray for us
Most honored of virgins	pray for us

The Rosary Prayer by Prayer

Chosen daughter of the Father	pray for us
Mother of Christ the King	pray for us
Glory of the Holy Spirit	pray for us
Virgin daughter of Zion	pray for us
Virgin poor and humble	pray for us
Virgin gentle and obedient	pray for us
Handmaid of the Lord	pray for us
Mother of the Lord	pray for us
Helper of the Redeemer	pray for us
Full of grace	pray for us
Fountain of beauty	pray for us
Model of virtue	pray for us
Finest fruit of the redemption	pray for us
Perfect disciple of Christ	pray for us
Untarnished image of the Church	pray for us
Woman transformed	pray for us
Woman clothed with the sun	pray for us
Women crowned with stars	pray for us
Gentle Lady	pray for us
Gracious Lady	pray for us
Our Lady	pray for us
Joy of Israel	pray for us
Splendor of the Church	pray for us
Pride of the human race	pray for us
Advocate of grace	pray for us
Minister of holiness	pray for us
Champion of God's people	pray for us
Queen of love	pray for us
Queen of mercy	pray for us
Queen of peace	pray for us

Additional Prayers Prayed with the Rosary

Queen of angels	pray for us
Queen of patriarchs and prophets	pray for us
Queen of apostles and martyrs	pray for us
Queen of confessors and virgins	pray for us
Queen of all saints	pray for us
Queen conceived without original sin	pray for us
Queen assumed into heaven	pray for us
Queen of all the earth	pray for us
Queen of heaven	pray for us
Queen of the universe	pray for us

Lamb of God, you take away the sins of the world	spare us, O Lord
Lamb of God, you take away the sins of the world.	hear us, O Lord
Lamb of God, you take away the sins of the world.	have mercy on us

Pray for us, O glorious Mother
of the Lord.
R. That we may become worthy
of the promises of Christ.

God of mercy,
listen to the prayers of your servants
who have honored your handmaid Mary
as mother and queen.
Grant that by your grace
we may serve you and our neighbor on earth
and be welcomed into your eternal kingdom.
We ask this through Christ our Lord.

R. Amen.

MAKING THE SIGN
OF THE CROSS

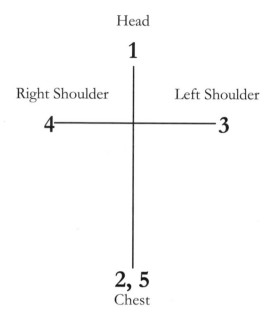

With your right hand:
1. Touch your forehead and say, "*In the name of the Father,*"
2. Touch your chest and say, "*and of the Son.*"
3. Touch your left shoulder and say, "*and of the Holy*"
4. Touch your right shoulder and say, "*Spirit.*"
5. Fold your hands in prayer and say, "*Amen.*"

THE PARTS OF THE ROSARY

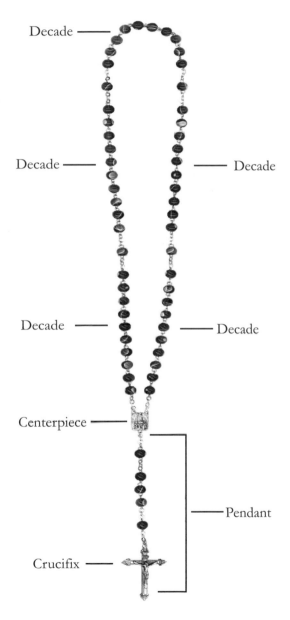

Decade

Decade

Decade

Decade

Decade

Centerpiece

Pendant

Crucifix

THE MAP OF THE ROSARY

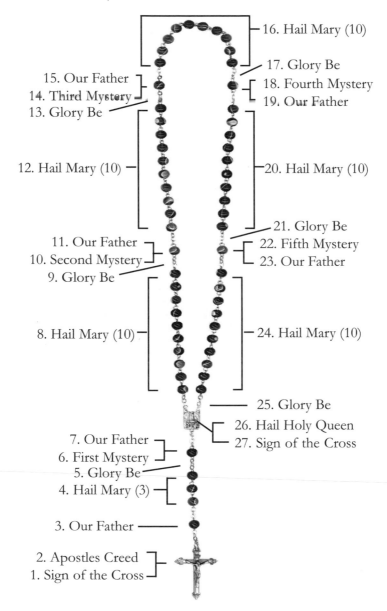

16. Hail Mary (10)

17. Glory Be

15. Our Father
14. Third Mystery
13. Glory Be

18. Fourth Mystery
19. Our Father

12. Hail Mary (10)

20. Hail Mary (10)

21. Glory Be
22. Fifth Mystery
23. Our Father

11. Our Father
10. Second Mystery
9. Glory Be

8. Hail Mary (10)

24. Hail Mary (10)

25. Glory Be
26. Hail Holy Queen
27. Sign of the Cross

7. Our Father
6. First Mystery
5. Glory Be
4. Hail Mary (3)

3. Our Father

2. Apostles Creed
1. Sign of the Cross

MARIAN ORGANIZATIONS

Association of Marian Helpers
  Eden Hill, Stockbridge, MA 01263
  http://www.marian.org/association/
The Association of the Miraculous Medal
  1811 West St. Joseph St., Perryville, MO 63775
  http://www.amm.org/
The Blue Army (World Apostolate of Fatima)
  Mt, View Rd, PO Box 976, Washington, NJ 07882
  http://www.bluearmy.com/
  Email: sercie@BLUEARMY.com
  Phone: 908-213-2223   Fax: 908-213-2263
The Cenacle of Our Lady of Divine Providence
  702 Bayview Ave.. Clearwater, FL 34619
  http://www.divineprovidence.org/Cenacle.htm
  Email: CenacleOfOurLady@aol.com
  Phone: 727-724-9505   Fax: 727-724-9421
Center for the Queen of Peace
  3350 Highway 6, Suite 412, Sugar Land, TX 77478
  http://www.marianland.com/centerfo.html
The Central Association of the Miraculous Medal
  475 E. Chelten Ave, Philadelphia, PA 19144-5785
  Phone: 1-800-523-3674   www.CAMMonline.org
Dominican Fathers
  http://www.rosary-center.org/
Eternal Word Television Network, Global Catholic Network
  http://www.ewtn.com/
Immaculate Heart of Mary Ministries
  12125 SE Laughin Water Rd. , Sandy, OR 97055
  http://www.ihomm.org/
  Phone: (503) 695-2468   Fax: (503) 695-6408
Intercessors of the Lamb Contemplative Formation Community
  4014 North Post Rd, Omaha, NE 68112
  http://www.bellwetheromaha.org/
Fr. Kolbe Missionaries of the Immaculata
  531 East Merced Ave, West Covina, CA 91790
  http://www.kolbemission.org/english/pagina_1_en.htm

Legion of Mary
    PO Box 1313, St. Louis, MO 63188
    http://www.legion-of-mary.ie/
Marian Renewal Ministry
    300 Newbury St., Boston, MA 02115-2805
    http://www.sign.org/marian/
    Phone: 617-266-7510; 617-267-1008 Ext 28
Militia of the Immaculata National Center
    1600 W. Park Ave., Libertyville, IL 60048
    http://www.consecration.com/
    Email: MI@consecration.com
    Phone: 847-367-7800, ext. 246   Fax: 847-367-7831
Missionary Oblates of Mary Immaculate
    9480 N. De Mazenod Drive, Belleville, IL 62223-1160
    http://www.oblatesusa.org
    Email: MAMI@oblatesusa.org
    Phone: 618-398-4848   Fax: 618-398-8788
Missionary Oblates of Mary Immaculate Lay Associations
    Sr. Geri Furmanek, ASC
Oblate Associates
    224 South De Mazenod Drive
    Belleville, IL 62223-1035
    http://www.omiusa.org/oblate_lay_associates.ht
Queen of the Americas Guild
    PO Box 851, St. Charles, IL 60174
    Phone: 630-584-1822

CONTACTS FOR FURTHER INFORMATION ON THE ROSARY

Dominican Fathers
    http://www.rosary-center.org/howto.htm
Immaculate Heart of Mary Ministries
    12125 SE Laughin Water Rd. , Sandy, OR 97055
    http://www.ihomm.org/
    Phone: (503) 695-2468   Fax: (503) 695-6408
Scriptural Meditations of the Rosary
    http://www.angelfire.com/electronic/rosary/luminous.html

ROSARIES FOR PURCHASE

Association of Marian Helpers
   Eden Hill, Stockbridge, MA 01263
   http://www2.marian.org/mhcstore
   Marian%20Rosary%20Sets.zhtml
Basilica of the National Shrine of the Immaculate Conception
   400 Michigan Ave., NE, Washington, D.C. 20017-1566
   Phone: 202-526-8300 Fax: 202-526-8313
The Central Association of the Miraculous Medal
   475 E. Chelten Ave, Philadelphia, PA 19144-5785
   1-800-523-3674, www.CAMMonline.org
   http://www.cammonline.org/pages/religiousArticles.html
Immaculate Heart of Mary Ministries
   12125 SE Laughin Water Rd. , Sandy, OR 97055
   http://www.ihomm.org/
   Phone: (503) 695-2468 Fax: (503) 695-6408
Intercessors of the Lamb Contemplative Formation Community
   4014 North Post Rd, Omaha, NE 68112
   http://www.bellwetheromaha.org/
Eternal Word Television Network, Global Catholic Network
   http://www.ewtn.com/
Theotokos Catholic Books Home Page
   http://www.theotokos.org.uk/
Rosary Mart.com
   http://www.rosarymart.com/.sc/ms/cat/1053363483994380/
   9/nc/Rosaries

GLOSSARY

Apocrypha: Biblical writings questioned as authentic in Jewish and Protestant Canons but some of which are accepted in the Roman Catholic Canon

Apostolic: the work of the apostles

Apparition: something that appears unexpectedly and in an unusual way such as a vision of Mary, Jesus, a saint, or an angel

Bible: also referred to as the Scriptures. The collection of sacred books, written by human beings but inspired by the Holy Spirit, which includes the Old and New Testaments and all or part of the Apocrypha

Book of Psalms (of David): 150 songs and poems attributed to David

Centerpiece: ornament or medal on the rosary beads

Chaplet: a string of beads or flowers sometimes used for counting prayers

Cohort: a group of people working or sharing a goal or mission such as a group of soldiers

Contemplate: to think about, ponder, or meditate upon something

Conversion: to change, transform. In the Christian context, a deliberate movement toward Jesus and the turning away from anything that prevents that journey toward Jesus

Corona: a crown or circle of items such as a circle of candles around an altar or prayer beads on a chain

Crucifix: a cross with a representation of Jesus' body

Decade: a section of the rosary consisting of a mystery, one Our Father, ten Hail Marys, and one Glory Be

Disciple: a student or follower of Jesus including all the baptized

Dogma: a teaching of the Church revealed by God that the faithful is required to believe

Doxology: a prayer of praise and glory to God

Encyclical: a teaching letter by the pope

Evangelization: the activity of proclaiming the gospels, the Good News of Jesus Christ

Incarnation: the fact that God the Son assumed a human body and soul becoming a true man while remaining true God. Jesus Christ is one person with two distinct natures

Glossary

Lord's Prayer: the prayer taught by Jesus and found in Matthew 6:9-13. Also referred to as the Our Father or *Pater Noster*

***Lumen Gentium*:** a document of the Second Vatican Council titled in English, "Dogmatic Constitution on the Church." The document covers issues under the chapter headings, The Mystery of the Church, The Call to Holiness, Religious, the Pilgrim Church, and Our Lady

Marian: anything referring to Mary such as a Marian Year, a year devoted to Mary

Meditate: to think about or reflect upon something

***Munificentissimus Deus*:** the declaration of the Dogma of the Assumption of Mary given on November 1, 1950 by Pope Pius XII

Nativity: the celebration of the birth, specifically the birth of Jesus as noted in the third Joyful Mystery

Papal bull: a document or Apostolic letter that bears the pope's seal of approval

***Pater Noster*:** Latin for "Our Father"

Pendant: the section of the rosary beads from the crucifix to the centerpiece

Praetoreum: the governor's office

Psalter: a collection of devotional hymns and prayers including the 150 psalms

Roman Breviary: The book of Divine Office, or Liturgy of the Hours, prayers to be read daily by priests

Salutation: a greeting or welcome

Scripture: sacred writing. The Bible

Theotokos: an official title for the Blessed Mother in recognition of her as the God-Bearer, the Mother of God. This title was given to Mary by the Council of Ephesus in the year 431

Tradition: oral and written teachings and practices of the Church

Visionary: a witness to an apparition

The Word: a term for the Bible or Holy Scriptures

BIBLIOGRAPHY

The Basilica of the National Shrine of the Immaculate Conception. *A Scriptural Rosary*. Washington, D.C.: The Basilica of the National Shrine of the Immaculate Conception, 2003.

Camille, Alice. *The Rosary. Mysteries of Joy, Light, Sorrow and Glory,* Chicago: ACTA Publications, 2003.

Knight, K. *The Catholic Encyclopedia*. Volume I. Online Edition: Robert Appleton Company, 2003. http://www.newadvent.org/cathen/

Groeschel, C.F.R., Benedict J. *The Rosary. Chain of Hope*. San Francisco: Ignatius Press, 2003.

Johnson, Elizabeth. *Truly Our Sister: A Theology of Mary in the Communion of Saints*. New York: Continuum International Publishing, 2003.

Lahey, Bishop Raymond J. *The Rosary of the Virgin Mary*. Ottawa, Canada: Novalis, Saint Paul University, 2003.

Libreria Editrice Vaticana. *Catechism of the Catholic Church*. Dubuque, IA: Brown-Roa, 1994.

Libreria Editrice Vaticana. *The Rosary of Pope John Paul II: The 20 Mysteries*. Vatican City: Vatican Press, 2002.

McKenna, Megan. *Praying the Rosary. A Complete Guide to the World's Most Popular Form of Prayer*. New York: Doubleday, 2004.

National Conference of Catholic Bishops. *Order of Crowning an Image of the Blessed Virgin Mary*. Washington D.C.: United States Catholic Conference, Inc., 1987.
John Paul II. Apostolic Letter, "On the Most Holy Rosary." October

Bibliography

16, 2002. Pauline Books & Media, 2002.

Sri, Edward. *The New Rosary in Scripture. Biblical Insights for Praying the 20 Mysteries.* Cincinnati: Servant Books, 2003.

Stravinskas, Ph.D., S.T.D., Peter M.J. *Catholic Dictionary.* Huntington, IN; Our Sunday Visitor, 2002.

Storey, William G. *A Prayer Book of Catholic Devotions.* Chicago: Loyola Press, 2004.

United States Conference of Catholic Bishops. *Mary in the Church. A Selection of Teaching Documents.* Washington, D.C.: United States Conference of Catholic Bishops, 2003.

Yeung, Andrew Jerome. *The Rosary. A Worried Parent Prays.* Toronto, Ontario, Canada: The Ave Maria Centre of Peace, 2000.

The Rosary Prayer by Prayer

INDEX

Index

215

Index

The Rosary Prayer by Prayer

Index

The Rosary Prayer by Prayer

Index

Index

Photo by Jim Spelman

MARY K. DOYLE has a conversational writing style as a result of nearly 35 years of experience writing advertising, electronic media, publicity, and newspaper articles. Her first book, *Mentoring Heroes*, received excellent reviews and is used by women studies programs and the mentoring field around the world.

Ms. Doyle has a Master of Arts Degree in Pastoral Theology from St. Mary-of-the-Woods College, Indiana and a Bachelor of Arts Degree in Business Management and Leadership from Judson College, Illinois. She is married, a mother of three adult children and four adult stepchildren.

JOSEPH CANNELLA is an accomplished artist with a specialty in graphite, silver point, and oil. His detailed illustrations and cover painting masterfully portray the human emotions and spirituality of the rosary. Perhaps most striking about Mr. Cannella's art is his unique perspective. Many of his renditions offer a viewpoint never seen before in the history of devotional art.

Photo by Jim Spelman

Mr. Cannella has a Bachelor of Fine Art Degree with a major in Life Drawing from the American Academy of Art, Chicago, Illinois.